HOW
TO READ
KARL MARX

HOW TO READ
KARL MARX

ERNST FISCHER

in collaboration with FRANZ MAREK

Translated by ANNA BOSTOCK

With an introduction and historical notes by
JOHN BELLAMY FOSTER

MONTHLY REVIEW PRESS
NEW YORK

Library of Congress Cataloging-in-Publication Data

Fischer, Ernst, 1899-1972.
    [Was Marx wirklich sagte. English]
    How to read Karl Marx / Ernst Fischer with Franz Marek ;
translated by Anna Bostock ; annotated by John Bellamy Foster. —
[New ed.]
        p. cm.
    Rev. ed. of: Marx in his own words. 1970.
    Includes index.
    ISBN 0-85345-974-6 (paper). — ISBN 0-85345-973-8 (cloth : alk. paper)
    1. Marx, Karl, 1818-1883. I. Marek, Franz. II. Foster, John Bellamy. III.
Fischer, Ernst, 1899-1972. Marx in his own words. IV. Title.
HX39.5.F5513 1995
335.43—dc20   95-33992
                                                                              CIP

Monthly Review Press
122 West 27th Street
New York NY 10001

Manufactured in the United States of America

10 9 8 7 6 5 4 3 2 1

CONTENTS

INTRODUCTION

John Bellamy Foster

It is one of the peculiar ironies of history that there are no limits to the misunderstanding and distortion of theories, even in an age when there is unlimited access to the sources; there is no more drastic example of this phenomenon than what has happened to the theory of Karl Marx in the last few decades. There is continuous reference to Marx and Marxism in the press, in the speeches of politicians, in books and articles written by respectable social scientists and philosophers; yet with few exceptions, it seems that the politicians and newspapermen have never as much as glanced at a line written by Marx, and that the social scientists are satisfied with a minimal knowledge of Marx. Apparently they feel safe in acting as experts in this field, since nobody with power and status in the social-research empire challenges their ignorant statements.

ERICH FROMM[1]

Karl Marx's reputation as one of the most influential thinkers of all time is unassailable. Modern social science would be inconceivable without him. Yet for anyone attempting to study Marx's thought under present circumstances, two problems immediately present themselves. First, Marx is not an easy read. His analysis is frequently complex, and his way of thinking foreign to those who have internalized the values and logic of this society. Many of today's readers will be unfamiliar with historical details that are taken for granted in much of Marx's work. Second, interpretations of Marx, to which readers might turn for help, are likely—more likely than in the case of most thinkers—to be systematically distorted; mixed, as Ernst Fischer says in the text that follows, "with propaganda of every kind."

7

During the cold war, Marx's ideas were deliberately falsified by both sides, often in quite similar and complementary ways. In the doctrines of the Communist regimes of the Soviet Union and Eastern Europe, Marx was reduced to a one-dimensional, dogmatic thinker—one who could be used to attack capitalism but who lacked any wider critical perspective that would make it possible to scrutinize those societies designating themselves as socialist. On the other side of the cold war divide, in the capitalist or free-market world, closely related misreadings of Marx's writings were advanced, though of an even more severe character, usually with the object of undermining his thought so as to blunt its criticism, while throwing doubt on any society or movement that drew upon his ideas.

These distortions have persisted in the era of free market triumphalism. Nowadays it is a given of common intellectual discourse that "Marx was wrong"—as if his ideas constituted nothing more than a set of failed predictions. What he had to say, we are encouraged to believe, is no longer of any direct importance, except in an antiquarian sense: we should read Marx much as we might read Plato. Again quoting Fischer, it is "necessary to put the *real* Marx against the distorted image so often presented of him." This is the main purpose of *How to Read Karl Marx*, Fischer's brief, classic account of Marx's thought, first published in Vienna in 1968 under the title *Was Marx wirklich sagte*—"What Marx Really Said."[2]

Ernst Fischer (1889-1972), an Austrian intellectual, editor, literary critic, and poet, was well qualified for the task of writing such a book. Fischer served as minister of education in Austria's post-World War II provisional government. He was also for many years a leading figure in the Austrian Communist Party. Fischer's politics, however, were always those of an independent Marxist, and he frequently broke with party discipline. He was influenced by the humanistic tradition within Marxism and wrote a major work entitled *The Necessity of Art: A Marxist Approach* (1961). In 1969, he was ousted from the party for his unequivocal denunciation of the 1968 Soviet invasion of Czechoslovakia. Fischer publicly declared that all European Communists were morally and politically bound to sever their ties with the Soviet leadership in Moscow. As an independent Marxist thinker, Fischer therefore stood outside the major ideological currents of the cold war. This independence of thought is clearly reflected in *How to Read Karl Marx*, and is shared by Fischer's collaborator, Franz Marek, another leading Austrian Communist and author of *Philosophy of World Revolution* (1966).[3]

Fischer's book on Marx is far from unique in its broad interpretation. It belongs to a vast body of literature on Marx and Marxism by disinterested inquirers after truth and independent radicals: work that is less known to the general public than the more widely disseminated cold war versions of Marx's thought. Yet Fischer's book stands out, even among the very best scholarly works on Marx, in its clarity, accuracy, brevity, and straightforward intelligence. As explained in the author's foreword, *How to Read Karl Marx* attempts to "let Marx speak for himself." But it recognizes that this raises challenges: "How much may we expect from the readers without making them lose heart?" Still, simplifying Marx carries its own dangers: "How much may we simplify without injury to Marx's greatness and originality?"

The present edition has been expressly designed to assist the reader in learning *how to* read Marx, incorporating additional supplementary material beyond what was provided in Fischer's original edition.

If Fischer's work makes distinctive contributions to the interpretation of Marx, they are to be found in his attempt to reaffirm what Marx actually said, in the face of such common misstatements of his views. Yet, Fischer addresses these distortions only indirectly through an affirmation of Marx's ideas. The purpose of this introduction is to fill this gap, by bringing out more explicitly the nature of the polemic against Marx, along with an exposition of some of most commonly distorted of Marx's ideas, designed to answer these standard criticisms.

Major misrepresentations of Marx are part of the general political culture, and readers are likely to carry them as part of their own unconscious intellectual baggage. Though pervasive, the nature of this anti-Marx propaganda is rarely addressed. There is no single source that is fully representative of the dominant set of criticisms of Marx's ideas. Yet nearly all such criticism follows a well-established pattern that has emerged over a century or more. As Jean-Paul Sartre noted (in *Search for a Method*, New York: Knopf, 1963), "an 'anti-Marxist' argument is only the apparent rejuvenation of a pre-Marxist idea."

Take for example certain editions of *The Communist Manifesto*. The *Manifesto* is considered a world classic, is required reading in many university classes, and is undoubtedly the most commonly read work by Marx (or Engels). It is not surprising, therefore, that the scholarly introductions to some of the most widely circulated editions of the *Manifesto* are in fact anti-introductions, whose purpose is to *undermine* the text—the direct opposite goal to that of most scholarly introductions to classic texts. Samuel Beer's 1955 introduction to the Crofts Classics edition of *The Communist Manifesto* and A.J.P. Taylor's 1967 introduction to the Penguin Books edition (both still in print) are two leading examples.[4]

As general editor of the Crofts Classics series published by Harlan Davidson, Harvard political scientist Samuel H. Beer himself elected to edit and introduce their edition of the *Manifesto*. Prior to this Beer had authored a cold war-style attack on Marx and Marxism in his book, *The City of Reason* (1949), in which he proclaims: "Marxist theory holds ... that conflicts of social interests can be settled, not by reflection and discussion, but only by violence"; and "Marxism holds that mind can only register ... what fact presents to it." Likewise, distinguished Oxford historian, essayist, and public commentator A.J.P. Taylor had made no secret of his own cold war anticommunism, or his antipathy to Marx and Marxism, prior to writing his introduction to the *Manifesto*. For example, in a 1956 review of G.D.H. Cole's *A History of Socialist Thought*, Taylor refers to "the Marxist scriptures," "Marx's advocacy of violent revolution," Marx's "failure to provide the equation demonstrating the collapse of capitalism," etc. Even before writing their introductions to *The Communist Manifesto*, both Beer and Taylor had therefore shown themselves to be sharply antagonistic toward Marx's ideas, to the point of abandoning all appearance of objectivity in this area.[5]

Both begin their introductions with the charge that Marxism is a religion. "Marxism," Beer informs us in his opening sentence, "... is a secular religion.... It is impossible to understand the deep appeal of the Marxist system unless we consider its powerful effect upon emotions which are essentially religious." "Marxism," Taylor likewise opines at the end of his first paragraph, "has become the accepted creed or religion for countless millions of mankind, and *The Communist Manifesto* must be counted as a holy book, in the same class as the Bible or the Koran."

Following this common starting point, Beer and Taylor develop their arguments in different ways, while agreeing on all the important details. Each tries to construct a straw version of Marx's historical materialism, that can then easily be knocked down. Marx emerges as a simplistic thinker who reduces all of human history to a single element, and then advocates immoral means of breaking with the present stage of history, and advancing his own, ill-conceived ends. Beer informs his readers at the outset that Marx's ideas rest on two propositions: (1) economic determinism, or the notion that (in Beer's words) "the economic structure of society ... develops independently of human will and thought ... [and] determines what takes place in other spheres of social life"; and (2) the idea that "the course of history is inevitably punctuated by violent revolutions." In Beer's account of Marx's historical materialist method, all social existence is reduced to "inexorable laws and must pass through certain definite stages," or modes of production. Each mode of production in history is strictly determined by the development of the physical forces of production, i.e., technology and economics.

Beer has Marx "rejecting with supreme scorn the view that it is thought which governs history." Instead, according to Beer, Marx promotes an abstract philosophical notion of a dialectical process within reality itself. This process, Beer tells us, boils down to a mechanical movement of thesis, antithesis, and synthesis governing all thought and/or events. A "thesis" (whether an idea or event) is opposed by its opposite, or an "antithesis," which leads inexorably to the development of a "synthesis" that supersedes both. Faith in the existence of such a mechanical movement, which operates independently of both the thoughts of individuals and human agency, is, according to Beer, the "pillar of the dogma of revolution." The implication is that Marx, despite his much-vaunted materialism, applied a closed, absolute certitude that only aped the very philosophical idealism that he rejected.

Beer's attempt to ridicule Marx's dialectical form of inquiry goes much further than this. Quoting Marx's statement from *The Poverty of Philosophy* that "the production relations of every society form a whole," Beer naively queries: "How can the parts ... form a whole ... and yet come into conflict with the whole?" By the same faulty reasoning one might as well ask: How can a family be a whole, and yet consist, as is frequently the case, of warring factions that come into conflict with one another and the entire family? Beer's mistake is to think that to refer to society (or the relations of production) *as a whole*, in the sense of being a definite complex of social relations, is at the same to time to contradict the notion of a *whole*, in the quite different sense of a completely unified and unitary entity. It is this kind of logical confusion that dialectical reasoning is expressly designed to avoid.

When he turns to Marx's economic ideas, Beer starts out by informing the reader that "the cornerstone of Marx's economics is the labor theory of value," and then tells us (as if the whole point of economic analysis could be reduced to this) "that the theory is hopeless as an attempt to explain prices, and in Marx's own lifetime it lost most of its adherents." Beer dismisses the term "exploitation," which was so central to Marx's critique of political economy as "heavy with moral condemnation" and suggesting "robbery"—as if such moral condemnation was at the heart of Marx's use of the term.

Beer's sharpest criticism of Marx's economics, however, is leveled at what he calls (following a well-established tradition among Marx-critics) the "theory of increasing misery." "The paradox—the central contradiction—of capitalism," according to Beer's rendition of Marx, "is that instead of benefiting from the process of accumulation, the workers, by that very process, are made even poorer and more miserable. This is the law of increasing misery which holds forth under capitalism as inexorably as the laws of accumulation and centralization." Hence, "workers," Beer writes purportedly summarizing Marx's views, are "unable to win higher wages and shorter hours." Beer objects: workers have repeatedly won such gains "throughout the last hundred years of capitalism"; Marx was misled by an undeveloped theory of economic crises to assume that the ranks of the unemployed would continually increase. "No more than a superficial knowledge of economic history," Beer wrote confidently in 1955 at the height of the post-World War II economic boom, "is needed to show how wildly out of accord with the facts the 'law' of increasing misery has proven to be." (In light of the unprecedented rise in world poverty in the decades since, even Beer's crude version of Marx seems more "in accord" with reality than Beer's own assertions.)

Like most establishment critics of Marx, Beer rests his case on the "base and superstructure" metaphor that Marx utilized in his 1859 "Preface to a Critique of Political Economy" (reprinted in the appendix to this volume). Here Marx *emphasizes* the material conditions of production (primarily the division of labor and class relations), which he sees as constituting the socioeconomic foundation or base that *conditions* (or delimits) other realms of social life, such as the state and religion. In the reductionist way in which Beer describes Marx's position, however, this is more than simply a case of theoretical emphasis. Rather we are told that for Marx, "there is one and only one chain of causation in history, the economic." Creative thinking, Beer declares, is entirely excluded "as an influence on history" in Marx's theory: "The whole subjective world of the mind is determined by the objective world of the economy." "Anyone will grant," he expounds, "that economic conditions 'affect' the thinking of the time ... and one of the most interesting tasks of intellectual history is to try to examine the relationship between thought and economics in particular periods. Marx, however, was not interested in framing interesting tasks for historians, but in stating a fundamental dogma of his revolutionary faith."

If that isn't enough to condemn Marx, his purported emphasis on "violent revolution" is. "In terms of the Marxian view of revolution," Beer tells us, "violence is the only way out." Indeed, "all elements in the Marxian system conspire to that conclusion." Marx's theory therefore constitutes "a dangerous vision" and "an invitation to tyranny," and "to teach that evil arises only from economic institutions is false." Having brought the reader to this conclusion, Beer's anti-introduction had thus fulfilled its purpose: the total repudiation of the text that the readers have before them—as well as, by implication, all other texts by Marx.

A.J.P. Taylor's introduction to the Penguin *Manifesto* twelve years after Beer's was even less restrained in its criticisms. For Taylor, Marx was a megalomaniac: "Marx never questioned, even in his time of total obscurity, that he was destined to be the intellectual master of the world." For the source of this supreme confidence Taylor looks to Marx's faith in his own dialectical method, which Taylor, like Beer, describes as a simple three-step system of thesis/antithesis/synthesis. According to Taylor, Marx's analysis pointed toward an absolute synthesis, marking the end of history, and ushering in what Taylor refers to as "an ideal society or Utopia where everyone would be happy without conflict for ever more." Marx's system, however, was flawed from the beginning since Marx "rigged his dialectic" by assuming that "men would behave as the social forces determined they should."

For Taylor, Marx's claims to have utilized "scientific" tools of investigation, and to have relied on historical analysis, were ludicrous. Marx, he says, "called his universal dogmas 'scientific'" even though he "never made a discovery in the scientific sense." In other words, the Marxist system was "a propagandist myth, deceptively adorned with scientific analysis." Likewise Taylor denies Marx's credentials as a historian: "In Marx's lifetime true history was beginning. He was not interested in it [the historical record]." Taylor's Marx, ignoring genuine science and history, placed too little emphasis on the evolution of society and too much on revolution, accepting the view "that the revolution would be short and sharp."

If Marx was a poor student of history, in Taylor's opinion, he was an even worse guide to economics. Ignoring the fact that *The Communist Manifesto* speaks of "the incessant revolutionization of the means of production"—that is, continual technological innovation—under capitalism, Taylor asserts: "Marx thought too narrowly in economic terms of capital and failed to allow for the endlessly stimulating effect of human invention." Further, "Marx regarded his discovery of the cause of [economic] crisis [in overproduction] as his greatest theoretical achievement. Unfortunately, his discovery rests on the assumption then held by all economists that 'labor' was the source of value. This assumption is no longer academically respectable." Marx's "prophecy" of growing economic contradictions for the system, we are told, has been proven false: "Increasing prosperity for the capitalists has everywhere brought with it increasing prosperity for the proletariat [those who survive by selling their labor power], instead of the increasing misery that Marx foretold." The "law of increasing misery," which Taylor (like Beer) attributes to Marx, is therefore invalid. The modern economic system, we are told, is no longer capitalistic, in Marx's sense. "There has been a divorce between ownership and control, which is altogether beyond Marx's system." "The profit motive," Taylor went so far as to contend, "has ceased to be the only driving force of capitalism, *or even the principal one*" (emphasis added).

Marx's revolutionary doctrine, as enunciated by Taylor, was little more than a call for violence under the leadership of dictatorial elements in the name of the proletariat. To be sure, Taylor admits, "Marx himself said that the socialist revolution might happen peacefully in Great Britain, the United States and perhaps Holland. Engels, later on, even added Germany." But all of this merely points to the fact that Marx "gradually gave up his entire revolutionary approach, without ever admitting that he had done so." Hence, insofar as Marx admitted the possibility of peaceful revolutions under certain favorable historical circumstances, he was, Taylor claims, simply abandoning his own revolutionary approach, which can be equated with violence.

Indeed, Marx's real tendency, Taylor contends, pointed in the direction not only of Stalin, but of Mussolini and Hitler as well. Taylor opines: "Marx's picture of the working class movement was of subservient and rather stupid workmen doing exactly what Marx told them." "The Fascist leaders ... were exactly of the type which Marx had postulated as leaders for the proletariat.... It only needed a spin of the coin to determine whether Mussolini would be a Communist or a Fascist, and, though Hitler never had Marxist leanings, he would have been at home a century earlier with the exiled tailors of the German Educational Workers' League" (an organization with which Marx and Engels were *indirectly* connected but which they pointedly declined to join).

Taylor concludes, the *Manifesto* was a work of religious fervor lacking rational meaning: "As with every religious book, men can find in *The Communist Manifesto* whatever they want to find." As for Marx himself, he was a "dogmatic optimist. He was convinced that events moved always toward the victory of the Higher. This faith in an inevitable outcome made him a great religious teacher."

Beer and Taylor paint their portraits of Marx so absolutely negatively that even those that doubt their overall accuracy might be inclined to think that there must be more than a germ of truth. This has contributed to the general acceptance of this type of broadside condemnation of Marx's method and works.

Paradoxically enough, this negative portrait of Marx's ideas, so pervasive within the anticommunist ideology of the West, resembled in certain key respects the interpretation to be found within the official Marxism of the Soviet Union. In Soviet ideology too, Marx was presented as an economic and technological determinist. Human agency, culture, and history itself were all downplayed in favor of a mechanical materialism. This vulgarization of Marx served a purpose: after Stalin's rise to power, official Soviet Marxism was increasingly used to defend a repressive social order. Uniformity of ideas was first encouraged, then demanded of would-be Marxists in the Stalin era. Marx's ideas were only deemed useful to the extent that they were deprived of all critical, subversive elements and reduced to a sterile collection of mechanical formulae, in which the economic (and technological) was rigidly separated from other aspects of life and seen as determinant. The "critical refutation of everything existing" prescribed by Marx was twisted into an uncritical acceptance of all terms and positions set by the political leadership of the Soviet Union, in both foreign and domestic politics. Yet many accepted the Soviet version of Marxism as a fulfillment and enhancement of Marx's ideas.

After Stalin's death and official disgrace, new theories introduced by Marxists from the academic domain, particularly in Western Europe, began to gain broader currency. Operating in isolation from the real world of class conflict and historical development, certain traditions within Western Marxism promoted interpretations of Marx's thought that, while not wholeheartedly Stalinist, were still antihumanist and antihistorical. The French philosopher Louis Althusser tried to extend Marx by interjecting the approach of structuralist thinkers like French anthropologist Claude Levi-Strauss. Taking Marx's concept of base and superstructure, which Marx used primarily as a metaphor for the relationship between the economic and the political, Althusser created a frozen structure in which human agency and history were absent, reducing Marxism to a set of formal abstractions. More recently, a new school of thought emerged from the Marxist intelligentsia: analytical Marxism. One proponent, G.A. Cohen, has argued that Marx's entire body of thought can be explained through an analysis of his base-superstructure metaphor, using the tools of analytical philosophy.

In both structuralist and analytical Marxism, the intellectual results have no practical use outside of academic inquiry.

Althusser presents much of his argument in a work called *For Marx*, while Cohen entitles his case *Karl Marx's Theory of History: A Defense*. Yet they both leave Marx reduced (albeit in Althusser's case "in the last instance") to a crude economic and technological determinist: exactly what Beer and Taylor claim about Marx and attack him for, Althusser and Cohen applaud and embrace.[6]

Critics who style themselves *post-Marxist*, claiming that their theoretical offerings subsume and transcend Marx's, have a history as old as Marxism itself. They tend to appear like mushrooms after a rainy season, every time a major event occurs that Marx failed to anticipate. None of these contributions have been able to break lasting new ground on the basis of their declared independence from Marxism. As Sartre observed, any such theory will be "at worst only a return to pre-Marxism; at best, only the rediscovery of a thought already contained in the philosophy which one believes he has gone beyond" (*Search for a Method*).

Such interpretations of Marx's materialist conception of history, which stress its supposedly deterministic and anti-humanistic elements, can be traced back to the Marxism of the Social Democratic movement (the Second International, based particularly in Germany) prior to World War I. This view of Marxism was promulgated at a time when less than half of what Marx had written had been published. The unpublished manuscripts included many of what have subsequently been seen as his most important works, including the *Critique of Hegel's Philosophy of Right* (written in 1843), *Economic and Philosophical Manuscripts (written in 1844), The German Ideology (written in 1846), and the Grundrisse* (or *Foundations for a Critique of Political Economy*, written in 1857-1858). These works did not appear in print until 1927 or after, and the *Grundrisse* in its entirety not before 1939. They received little attention until the late 1940s, and did not appear (for the most part) in English until the 1960s and 1970s. Yet it is these writings that bring out most fully the understanding of the humanity that resides in all human beings (or "man" as a generic species, in the rhetoric of Marx's era) at the foundation of Marx's thought.[7]

The gradual publication of the remainder of Marx's works thus helped spark a humanistic reinterpretation of his thought that reached its height in 1968, a year of revolt in both

East and West. Fischer's little book, published that very year, begins with Marx's humanism: his conception of labor as the creative expression of human needs and powers, and his analysis of the alienation of human creativity in class society. For Marx, the goal of development, Fischer tells us, "was positive humanism, the real life of man." This humanistic perspective was reflected in Marx's famous passage on religion in which he said not simply that "religion ... is the opium of the people" but much more: "Religion is the sigh of the oppressed creature, the sentiment of a heartless world, and the soul of soulless conditions. It is the *opium* of the people."[8] Rather than a one-sided repudiation of religion, Marx both praised and condemned religion from a historical materialist standpoint, one that placed its primary emphasis on the developmental needs of the majority of humankind.*

Marx's emphasis on dialectical reasoning, which was inspired in part by the earlier work of the German philosopher Georg Wilhelm Friedrich Hegel (1770-1831), was inseparably connected to this humanistic thrust of his thought. Rather than a mechanistic concept of thesis/antithesis/synthesis, a common vulgarization of Hegel's approach, Fischer explains that the dialectic concentrates on "the inner contradiction within the nature of thought and of all things, the recognition that nothing can be understood in isolation or as a rectilinear sequence of cause and effect, but only as the multiple interaction of all factors and being in conflict with itself: that everything, as it comes into being, produces its own negation and tends to progress towards the negation of the negation."

The root notion of dialectic can be traced to the ancient Greeks. The early Greek philosopher Heraclitus wrote of the identity of opposites and of the negative that was positive: "War is the father and king of all things.... Opposition is

---

* Marx's critique of religion overlaps in certain respects with the viewpoint of contemporary liberation theology. See, for example, Gustavo Gutierrez, *A Theology of Liberation* (New York: Orbis Books, 1973). As Fischer notes, Marx extended his critique of religion to the critique of atheism, insofar as it attempts to assert the existence of humanity by negating god. For Marx, such atheism was "no longer meaningful," since socialism is rooted in the direct perception of humanity's real world conditions.

good.... Men do not understand that what is divided is consistent with itself, it is a harmony of tensions. ... the fairest harmony comes out of difference; everything originates in strife.... We enter and do not enter the same rivers, we are and are not." But the modern notion of dialectic, as propounded by nineteenth-century thinkers like Hegel and Marx, was tied to Enlightenment conceptions of history and development. "The True is the whole," Hegel wrote. "But the whole is nothing other than the essence consummating itself through its development." Dialectical thinking was thus a way of grasping the complexity of change in a world where social relations interpenetrated, where all was in flux, and where the potential of anything in history could be discovered only in the process of its development.[9]

Although not in itself constituting some infallible formula for truth, dialectical reasoning can sharpen awareness of the instability and impermanence of all social relations, revealing the ways in which they are, in the last analysis, one-sided, partial, particular, and finite. In Hegel's words:

> Wherever there is movement, wherever there is life, wherever anything is carried into effect in the actual world, there Dialectic is at work. It is also the soul of knowledge which is truly scientific. In the popular way of looking at things, the refusal to be bound by the abstract deliverances of understanding appears as fairness, which, according to the proverb Live and Let live, demands that each should have its turn; we admit the one, but we admit the other also. But when we look more closely, we find that the limitations of the finite do not merely come from without; that its own nature is the cause of its abrogation, and that by its own act it passes into its counterpart. We say, for instance, that man is mortal, and seem to think that the ground of his death is in external circumstances only; so that if this way of looking were correct, man would have two special properties, vitality and—also—mortality. But the true view of the matter is that life, as life, involves the germ of death, and the finite, being radically self-contradictory, involves its own self-suppression.[10]

As Marx wrote in *Capital*, there was a "rational kernel within the mystical shell" of the Hegelian dialectic. "In its rational form," he wrote,

> the dialectic is an abomination to the bourgeoisie and its doctrinaire spokesmen, because it includes in its positive understanding of what exists a simultaneous recognition of its negation, its inevitable destruction; because it regards every historically developed form as being in a fluid state, in motion, therefore grasps its transient aspect

as well; and because it does not let itself be impressed by anything, being in its very essence critical and revolutionary.[11]

The central concept of dialectical reasoning is *contradiction*. In the dialectical viewpoint all phenomena are understood to be relations, which interpenetrate with other relations, and which can be understood in terms of processes, usually of a developmental character. Contradiction, in this context, to quote New York University political theorist Bertell Ollman, means nothing other than "the incompatible development of different elements within the same relation, which is to say, between elements which are also dependent on each other." For example, the abstract concept of *the family* is made more concrete and meaningful if understood as a complex set of relations (between cohabiting partners, parents and children, siblings, income-earners and dependents within the family, etc.). Such relations are constantly changing and developing and thus are made incompatible with each other, both within the family and as a result of its interaction with the larger world of social intercourse at a particular point in history. Dialectical reasoning therefore moves one beyond viewing the family as a static entity, and toward the analysis of it in terms of its inner dynamic and contradictions.

According to the dialectical perspective, not only impermanence but also *radical qualitative breaks in development* are to be expected. A historical socioeconomic system like capitalism could, Marx believed, be best understood in terms of "the contradictory, socially determined feature of its elements" that constitute its "predominant characteristic." The mistake of most mainstream liberal (or bourgeois) social science is that it attempts to "exorcise contradiction" each time it is presented by the system, rather than analyzing it as a feature produced by the system's own development. As a result, the historical and changing character of capitalism is often missed altogether.[12]

Another distortion by some would-be Marxists and anti-Marxists attributes to Marx a rigid designation of the political and ideological as spatially distinct spheres, with these and all other spheres subordinated or reduced in the end to the economic (and technological) base. Marx's critique of political economy was in fact directed at demonstrating how the economic could be understood *in terms of* political and social relations, thus breaking down any sense of strict separation of the economic and political, other than what was produced in contradictory form by capitalist society itself. "Marx's radical innovation on bourgeois political economy," noted Ellen Meiksins Wood, a political science professor at York University, Toronto, "was precisely to define the mode of production and economic laws themselves in terms of 'social factors.'"[13]

Nor did Marx see history merely as a straight line of predetermined modes of production, each brought into being and governed by economic forces. He objected forcefully to attempts in his own time to reduce his analysis to a set of rigid abstractions and mechanical formulae that could be substituted for genuine historical inquiry. In the *Communist Manifesto* itself Marx and Engels observed that class struggle in history has "each time ended either in a revolutionary reconstitution of society at large, or in the common ruin of the contending classes." Regression as well as progress was therefore conceivable, though Marx and Engels (like most revolutionaries) were optimists, and hence frequently wrote as if genuine human progress were inevitable.[14]

Marx argued, in a set of hypotheses that he described as "the guiding thread" of his studies, that the growth of human productive forces is a social potential inscribed within the nature of human productive activity itself. Yet every given stage of development of the productive forces of society—that is, of the human species, and of the division of labor—is bound up historically with certain social relations of production, particularly class relations. Once a particular form of class domination comes into existence as a result of this complex process of historical development, the dominant element in the relation attempts to freeze it into place, and the existing society loses its progressive character. Despite changes in the material conditions of production, any ruling class will seek to preserve its rule at all cost, thus becoming a fetter on further social and economic development. The state, law, religion, and the entire realm of ideas, to the extent that they represent the overarching interests in society and are conditioned by the underlying set of socioeconomic relations, will all be enlisted for the purpose of defending the status quo and of patching up society's contradictions—*ultimately*, Marx believed, *to no avail*. As a result of this growing incompatibility between the forces and relations of production social conflict is intensified and a revolutionary situation emerges. In Marx's words, "At a certain stage of their development, the material productive forces of society come in conflict with the existing relations of production, or—what is but a legal expression for the same thing—with the property relations within which they have been at work hitherto. From forms of development of the productive forces these relations turn into fetters. Then begins an epoch of social revolution."[15]

The great bourgeois revolutions against feudalism—the English and French revolutions, in particular—had assumed this general character. Moreover, the development of bourgeois society, Marx believed, prepared the way for the emergence of new contradictions, separating the social forces and relations of production, and resulting in an age of revolutionary struggle in which the working class would be the main protagonist. Since this would involve the revolt of the great majority of humankind, it would embody a democratic potential greater than any that had preceded it, leading society in the direction of genuine democracy—a classless society.

Marx sought to demonstrate not only how capitalist society functions but also how historical conditions would allow social forces to intervene in this process and supersede it.

Recognizing the full complexity of class relations in society, he abstracted from what he regarded as the less essential aspects of the social process in order to draw out more clearly the core relations. Then, by a process of *successive approximations*, he attempted to move to more and more concrete and empirical levels of analysis. Referring to Marx's method, Paul Sweezy (see appendix, "Marx's Method") describes "the legitimate purpose of abstraction in social science," which "is never to get away from the real world but rather to isolate certain aspects of the real world for intensive investigation." As Marx himself wrote in the preface to *Capital*, "In the analysis of economic forms, neither microscopes nor chemical reagents are of assistance. The power of abstraction must replace both."[16]

In Volume I of *Capital*, Marx applied this method to portray capitalism in its purest form: the relation of the capitalist class to the working class, abstracting from all other class (and social) relations. This procedure has led some critics to accuse Marx of having ignored the broader range and variety of class relations and individual interactions.* Nevertheless, in his more concrete historical writings (such as *Class Struggles in France*, *The Eighteenth Brumaire of Louis Bonaparte*, and *The Civil War in France*), Marx was extremely careful to take account of the many forms of social interaction. As Fischer writes, Marx "does not, when carrying out a concrete analysis, overlook the multitude of 'middle and intermediate classes' between the bourgeoisie and proletariat, or the possibility of all kinds of alliances in the class struggle."

In concentrating on the analysis of the laws of motion of capital and the capitalist class/working class relation, Marx was not trying to impose a fixed formula that made all further analysis unnecessary. Just the opposite: his theory serves to uncover the main tendencies marking the current phase of historical development as a starting point for analyzing the period in its full complexity. He sought to reveal the hidden world of real human beings and their productive relations that commodity fetishism subsumed to the inanimate world of things and disembodied ideas.

Under capitalism everything appears on the surface to be based on equality—the exchange of equivalents on the market. Workers enter into a labor contract with their employers in which they sell their labor power for wages or salaries that reflect the historically determined value of their labor power (the accepted level of subsistence). This system was compared by Marx to a Garden of Eden of the "innate rights of man":

> It is the exclusive realm of Freedom, Equality, Property, and Bentham [an eighteenth-century Utilitarian philosopher]. Freedom because both buyer and seller of a commodity, let us say of labor-power, are determined only by their free will. They contract as free persons, who are equal before the law. Their contract is the final result in which their joint will finds a common legal expression. Equality, because each enters into relation with the other, as a simple owner of

---

* Beginning with the German Social Democrat Eduard Bernstein, critics have perpetuated the myth that Marx presented a thesis of the gradual "disappearance of the middle classes." For a thorough critique of this myth see Hal Draper, *Karl Marx's Theory of Revolution*, vol. II, *The Politics of Social Classes* (New York: Monthly Review Press, 1978), pp. 613-27.

commodities, and they exchange equivalent for equivalent. Property, because each disposes only of what is his own. And Bentham, because each looks only to his own advantage.[17]

Digging deeper, however, Marx finds the real basis of the accumulation of wealth and profits under capitalism not within this Eden of exchange, but only at the level of production itself—the transformation of raw materials into commodities through labor. Marx therefore invites the reader of *Capital* to follow him and the owner of money "into the hidden abode of production, on whose threshold hangs the notice 'No admittance except on business.'"[18]

Through a detailed analysis that focuses on the factory system already emerging in the late nineteenth century, Marx breaks down the underlying means through which profit is extracted from labor in the production process.* He explains that the value-added (net income) created during a day's work can be divided into variable capital (or wages) and surplus value (or gross profits). During the first portion of the working day, a worker produces the value equivalent of his/her labor power or wages. The worker does not go home at that point, however, but instead continues to work for the remainder of the working day. The residual, surplus value produced during this remaining portion of the working day provides the gross profits of the owner of the means of production. The ratio of the second part of the working day to the first is the ratio of gross profits to wages, or, in Marx's terms, of surplus value to variable capital, S/V. Marx called this the *rate of exploitation*— a term he used dispassionately, in a way similar to a modern geologist speaking of the exploitation of natural resources.

It is the main aim of each individual capitalist enterprise within the production process to raise the rate of exploitation, that is, to decrease the portion of total working time necessary

---

* Modern economists disagree about the validity of the labor theory of value of classical economics, which is applied in all of Marx's economic theory. Nevertheless, the labor theory of value (and classical value analysis more generally) still has many able defenders among radical economists—those outside of the dominant tradition of neoclassical economics. See Sweezy, *The Theory of Capitalist Development*, and Duncan Foley, *Understanding Capital: Marx's Economic Theory* (Cambridge, MA: Harvard University Press, 1986).

to reproduce the wages of the workers. At the last turn of the century, lengthening the working day—"the stretch-out"— was standard practice. (That is, until the industrial work force emerging around the world organized and waged pitched battles—including strikes, sabotage, and mass confrontations with the police and army—to institutionalize a shorter workday. Before that time, the very idea of an eight-hour day was considered outrageously subversive in U.S. society.) The stretch-out increases the surplus portion of the working day and the profits of the owner of the means of production without altering the level of wages or productivity.

Nowadays, however, management prefers to rely on "the speed-up," or driving down unit labor costs by increasing labor productivity, which reduces the portion of the working day that must be devoted to producing the value equivalent of the wages of the workers. This requires a more detailed management of the labor process itself, and the systematic, ever-increasing alienation of the workers from the process of production. By these means more and more workers are made mere appendages to machines, while others become "redundant" and can be discharged. The displaced workers join the industrial "reserve army" of the unemployed; the greater the supply of jobless workers, the greater competition for a limited number of jobs, and the lower the wages. This ensures that workers are able to gain little or nothing as a result of the increases in labor productivity, sometimes even seeing their real wages (wages adjusted for inflation) fall. The war between capitalists and workers, Marx states, "has the peculiarity that its battles are won less by recruiting than by discharging the army of labor."[19]

The surplus value appropriated by the owner of the means of production (whether an individual, a family, or a corporation) forms the basis of the accumulation of *capital* (private wealth) on an ever-expanding scale, and its aggregation in fewer and fewer hands. For the capitalist (seen as a mere "personification" of capital), Marx wrote, "Accumulate, accumulate! That is Moses and the prophets!" But the possession of ever greater wealth by the few is accompanied by the growth of the dispossessed sectors of society. Unlike conservatives, who see in accumulated wealth the beginning of prosperity that will someday "trickle down" to the have-not majority, or liberals, who propose government controls and uplift programs in the context of business as usual, Marx reveals the growth of relative wealth and relative poverty side by side as a reflection of the contradictory nature of capitalist society itself. According to what he called "the absolute general law of capitalist accumulation":

> In proportion as capital accumulates the situation of the worker, be his payment high or low, must grow worse.... [T]he law which always holds the relative surplus population or industrial reserve army in equilibrium with the extent and energy of accumulation rivets the worker to capital more firmly than the wedges of Hephaestus held Prometheus to the rock. It makes an accumulation of misery a necessary condition, corresponding to the accumulation of wealth. Accumulation of wealth at one pole is therefore, at the same time accumulation of misery, the torment of labor, slavery, ignorance, brutalization and moral degradation at the opposite pole, i.e. on the side of the class that produces its own product as capital.[20]

This argument has often been termed Marx's "theory of increasing misery." Marx, however, never employed this term. It is true that in his earliest consideration of the wage question, Marx, in the words of the economist Ernest Mandel, envisioned "a tendency for wages to decline toward the physiological minimum living wage and stay there." Yet in his mature political economic writings, most notably *Capital*, he adopted a more dialectical view, arguing that although the real wages of workers might rise with accumulation, this would necessarily be accompanied by a growing relative disparity (increasing polarization) between capitalist and worker—a disparity that would become greater whether the wages of the workers be "high or low."[21]

Marx was very conscious of growing human misery and social polarization, but in a much more complex way than is usually attributed to him. "Our desires and pleasures," he wrote, "spring from society; we measure them, therefore, by society and not by the objects which serve for their satisfaction. Because they are of a social nature, they are of a relative nature." Greater relative disparities were what ultimately counted in human society. Moreover, Marx frequently pointed to extreme conditions of *global* inequality that result principally from capitalism.

The force of this argument should be even more apparent today. At present a billion people are below the household poverty line—designated by the World Bank as a per capita household income of $370 per year or less (in 1985 prices).

Malnutrition and starvation are common. Subsistence and below subsistence wages, as well as unemployment and underemployment rates of 50 percent or more, are common in countries on the periphery of the world economy.

Meanwhile, in the advanced economies—where even Fischer (writing in 1968) takes exception with Marx's perspective—the promise of equality of conditions has evaporated. In the United States, a mere 1 percent of the population in 1989 owns over 48 percent of total financial wealth (which can be equated with ownership of the means of production), while the bottom 80 percent owns only 6 percent of such wealth—a disparity that has been increasing rather than decreasing over recent decades. A widening gap between the haves and have-nots is therefore setting in on a global scale.[22]

Marx was convinced that the contradictions of capitalist society would in time make it insupportable. Workers would revolt; the expropriators would be expropriated. This was more than a mere dream. Revolts led by working classes did occur. The most famous of these in Marx's own lifetime was the Paris Commune of 1871. As a rule, such rebellions were suppressed by military force. The Communards were crushed by the military forces of the French state in May 1871 in one of the bloodiest instances of state terrorism in recorded history.

This historical context is the key to understanding Marx's position with respect to the revolutionary recourse to violence. Rather than an advocate of violence as such, Marx was an advocate of social revolution, which could, he believed, take either peaceful or violent forms: "We must declare to the governments: we know that you are the armed power which is directed against the proletariat; we shall proceed against you by peaceful means where possible, and by force of arms if necessary"—necessity in this latter case arising from the actions of the armed forces of the state itself.

There is a direct connection between the "violent revolution" controversy and Marx's equally controversial use of the term "dictatorship of the proletariat." The term was not invented by Marx, but he, like many French socialists of his time, adopted it to describe the form of transitional government he anticipated would immediately follow a successful working class revolution.

Twentieth century critics have frequently used this reference to "dictatorship" as evidence that Marx favored totalitarian rule. Thus David Caute opines: "Probably proletarian dictatorship implied a harsher, post-revolutionary concentration of power than mere working-class rule." Such interpretations typically ignore the change in meaning of *dictatorship* since the nineteenth century, when the term was still being used in its classical Latin sense. Henry R. Spencer in the *Encyclopaedia of the Social Sciences* (1931) writes: "Dictatorship is a term which has undergone notable change of meaning." Until recently, Spencer observed, the term *dictatorship* has been kept separate from other terms (such as *absolutism, despotism* and *tyranny*) and "history has used it to designate emergency assumption of power.... In the decade following the [First] World War, however, there was a widespread tendency to use the term dictatorship as synonymous with absolutism or aristocracy." In classical Rome, the institution known as the *dictatura* was part of the constitution and was legal. It allowed for the temporary assumption of power by a one-man ruler in a period of emergency when the state was endangered. Such constitutional arrangements were similar to the modern phenomenon of martial law or a state of siege.[23]

For Marx, the dictatorship of the proletariat thus represented an embattled transitional stage in the movement toward communist society—the latter to be governed by the principle "from each according to his ability, to each according to his needs." True democracy or communism as framed by Marx required not the rule of the proletariat over the bourgeoisie, but elimination of classes altogether. Speculating on the early period of the transition to communism, the new society, Marx suggested, would be "still stamped with the birthmarks of the old society from whose womb it emerges." Although more democratic than earlier forms of society, in the sense of being the rule of the majority class, Marx's dictatorship of the proletariat remains a "dictatorship"—in the triple sense of being embattled, transitional, and not yet fully democratic—but free to develop into a much wider democracy once the initial period of revolutionary transformation has been completed.

Marx regarded the Paris Commune, which implemented universal suffrage, the right of immediate recall of elected representatives at all times, and a limitation of the salary levels of officials to that of ordinary workers, as constituting the first such form of workers' government. "Freedom," Marx declared in *Critique of the Gotha Programme*, with the experience of the Commune in mind, "consists in converting the state from an organ superimposed upon society into one completely subordinate to it ... the forms of the state are more free or less free to the extent that they restrict the 'freedom of the state.'" He went on to complain of the tendency of some socialists to substitute "a servile belief in the state," i.e., in "the government machinery" separated from the rest of society, for the rule of the people. The revolutionary political significance of the Paris Commune, Marx insisted in *The Civil War in France*, lay in:

> the destruction of the State power which claimed to be the embodiment of ... unity independent of, and superior to, the nation itself.... While the merely repressive organs of the old governmental power were to be amputated [in the Communal Constitution], its legitimate functions were to be wrested from an authority usurping pre-eminence over society itself, and restored to the responsible agents of society.

Indeed, the constitution of the Paris Commune, Marx wrote, represented nothing less than "the tendency of a government of the people by the people"—"the political form at last discovered in which to work out the economic emancipation of labor."[24]

Another widespread myth equates Marxism with power-grabbing by small groups. In fact, Marx was always opposed to the "conspiratorial putschism" associated with French revolutionaries like Auguste Blanqui. Nothing was more alien to Marx than the Blanquist notion that a revolution could be completed in twenty-four hours—a statement made by Blanqui that Taylor quotes in his introduction to the *Manifesto*, implying that Marx too held this view. Strongly condemning such conspiratorial approaches to revolution, Marx wrote:

> Their business consists precisely in forestalling the process of revolutionary development, pushing it artificially to crisis, making a revolution impromptu, without the preconditions for a revolution. The sole preoccupation of revolution, for them, is the adequate organization of their conspiracy. They are the alchemists of revolution, and they entirely share the earlier alchemist's disorder of ideas and narrow-mindedness in fixed conceptions.[25]

For Marx, revolutions were long processes that demanded the right preconditions and mass action. They had nothing in common with mere insurrectionism rooted in conspiratorial organizations.

Indeed, there was nothing rigid or narrow about Marx's approach to the world, either in theory or practice. In theory he opposed dogmas of every kind. Marx's favorite motto was *De omnibus dubitandum*—"Doubt everything"; his favorite maxim was "Nothing human is alien to me." He argued for a "*ruthless criticism of everything existing*: ruthless in two senses: The criticism must not be afraid of its own conclusions, nor of conflict with the powers that be." In response to the narrow conceptions of some of those who purported to be his followers in his own lifetime, Marx once quipped in a semi-humorous vein, "I am not a Marxist." Rather than avoiding empirical questions by adhering fixedly to strict conclusions, Marx altered his views on numerous occasions as more historical information became available, and where changed conditions demanded a changing analysis. Political practice was not an empty field on which narrow theoretical conclusions were imposed from on high, but the means of discovering the validity of one's knowledge, and at the same time the key to new theoretical discoveries which could provide new guidelines for practice.

In line with this, Marx demonstrated again and again that he was able to learn from the vernacular of indigenous revolutionary movements, and to alter (or enlarge) his own theory and practice accordingly.[26]

Marx's ideal was of a world in which each human being would be creatively linked to the rest of humanity and to nature; a world in which ordinary individuals would live a many-sided existence and would have a wealth of connections, not because they *had* much but because they *were* much; a world in which the full development of the individual was the basis for the full development of society, and vice versa. It was an ideal that Marx, as a revolutionary optimist, was convinced would be increasingly approximated in time as a result of the continuing struggle of the direct producers to remake the conditions of human history. This emphasis on the making and remaking of history by human beings in the interest of a more universal humanity—one in which the lives of untold numbers of individuals would no longer be crippled for the benefit of a very few—is Marx's great gift to the world, giving Marxism its enduring quality as the revolutionary humanist philosophy *par excellence*.[27]

BIOGRAPHICAL DATA

1818
May 5: Karl Heinrich Marx born at Trier, the son of Heinrich Marx, a solicitor. The elder Marx, who came from an old family of rabbis, had adopted Christianity a year previously.

1830-1835
After a childhood spent in an atmosphere of prosperity and culture, Karl Marx attends Trier's Friedrich-Wilhelm-Gymnasium (a Jesuit high school) for a period of five years. His intellectual development is encouraged by his father, who has a lively interest in philosophy, and by State Councillor Ludwig von Westphalen, with whom he reads the Greek poets and Shakespeare.

1835-1841
Attends Bonn University and, after two terms, Berlin University, where he reads law, philosophy, and history. As a student, Marx makes excerpts from Aristotle, Spinoza, Leibniz, Hume, and Kant, and writes some romantic poems, a fragment of a tragedy, and a few chapters of a novel in the manner of Laurence Sterne. In 1836 he becomes engaged to Jenny von Westphalen, his older friend's daughter. Increasingly influenced by Hegel's philosophy, he becomes associated with a student circle of Young Hegelians, a left-wing tendency, at the university. Clashes with his father, who is alarmed by the young Marx's passionate nature, lack of moderation, and financial carelessness.

1838
Father dies on May 10.

1841
Doctorate awarded in recognition of his thesis on *The Difference Between the Democritean and Epicurean Philosophies of Nature*. Moves to Bonn in hopes of securing a teaching post at the university.

1842
Abandons teaching ambitions upon the political suspension from Bonn University of his friend and teacher Bruno Bauer. Joins staff of liberal paper

31

Rheinische Zeitung of Cologne. Becomes editor-in-chief on October 15 and moves to Cologne. November 16: Meets Frederick Engels, who had written articles for *RZ*, when Engels, the son of a manufacturer of Barmen and two years younger than Marx, visits the *RZ* office on his way to England for business training.

1843   March 18: Leaves the paper on account of increasing difficulties with the censorship office. Marries Jenny von Westphalen on June 19. Begins reading intensively in the history of the French Revolution. Moves to Paris at the end of October; edits radical *Deutsch-Französische Jahrbücher* together with Arnold Ruge. *Critique of Hegel's Philosophy of Right*; *On the Jewish Question.*

1844   Start of close collaboration with Engels. Publishes Engels's *Outlines of a Critique of Political Economy* in *Jahrbücher*. Contacts with Heinrich Heine, French socialists, and the proletariat. Begins systemic study of the classics of political economy. *Economic and Philosophical Manuscripts.*

1845   Expelled from France at the demand of the Prussian government. Moves to Brussels and is joined by Engels shortly thereafter. *The Holy Family.* Visits London and Manchester with Engels. Renounces Prussian citizenship as a result of harassment in Brussels by the Prussian government. Financial troubles, which are to persist until the end of his life.

1846   *The German Ideology* completed, on which Marx and Engels had begun work at the end of 1845. *Theses on Feuerbach.* Contacts with the English Chartists and the League of the Just.

1847   *The Poverty of Philosophy.* Debate with Proudhon. Collaboration with the Communist League. Participation in the second congress of the League, held in London. Gives series of lectures to the German Workers Association in Brussels, published two years later as *Wage-Labor and Capital.*

1848   February: the *Communist Manifesto.* Revolution in France. In early March, expelled from Brussels. Revolutions in Germany, Hungary, and Austria. Marx and Engels in Cologne. On May 31, first issue of the *Neue Rheinische Zeitung* with Marx as editor-in-chief. Dissolution of the Communist League.

1849	Marx is accused of incitement to armed rebellion but acquitted by a Cologne jury. On May 16, after the triumph of the counter-revolution, he is expelled as a "stateless" person. The last issue of the *Neue Rheinische Zeitung* appears on May 18. Arrival in Paris, June 3; beginning of exile in London, August 24.
1850	*The Class Struggles in France.* Refounding of the Communist League. *Neue Rheinische Zeitung, Politisch-Ökonomische Revue* is launched, but has to cease publication after five issues. Split in the League. Engels returns to his family business in Manchester to help support Marx's work and himself.
1851	Begins contributing to *New York Daily Tribune*. First series of articles later known as *Revolution and Counterrevolution in Germany*, written by Engels under Marx's name.
1852	*The Eighteenth Brumaire of Louis Bonaparte.* October and November: trial of communists in Cologne. Seven of the accused are given three to six years in jail, four are acquitted. Final dissolution of the League.
1853	*Revelations About the Cologne Communist Trial.*
1855-1862	Writes hundreds of articles for *New York Daily Tribune, Neue Oder-Zeitung*, Urquhart's *Sheffield Free Press*, Jones's *People's Paper* and *Wiener Presse*, and *Das Volk.* Constant poverty and ill health. Jenny Marx suffers nervous breakdowns. Engels gives continual assistance.
1859	*A Contribution to The Critique of Political Economy.* Political differences with Ferdinand Lassalle, with whom Marx has been acquainted since 1848. Lassalle's view that the liberal bourgeoisie, rather than the Junkers, the militarist Prussian ruling class, are the principal enemy in Germany becomes increasingly the main subject of disagreement.
1861	Marx and Lassalle meet in Berlin. American Civil War begins.
1863	*Theories of Surplus Value.* Lassalle's agitational and organizational activities in Germany reach their climax.
1864	August 31: Lassalle dies after being fatally wounded in a duel. September 28: Founding of the First International in London, union of all tendencies within the labor movement—trade unionists, communists, socialists, anarchists. Marx is elected as one of the thirty-two

members of the General Council. The program outlined in his inaugural address is unanimously adopted.

1865   Breaks with the General German Workers Association founded by Lassalle. Conference of the International in London. *Wages, Price, and Profit.*

1866   First Congress of the International in Geneva.

1867   *Capital*, Volume I. Second Congress of the International in Lausanne.

1868   Third Congress of the International in Brussels.

1869   Fourth Congress of the International in Basel. Open clash between Marx and Michael Bakunin, the theoretician of anarchism and leader of the International Alliance of Socialist Democrats; no decision is reached. Congress of the German Social-Democratic Workers' Party at Eisenach.

1870   Franco-Prussian War. *Addresses of the General Council of the International on the Franco-Prussian War.* Engels moves to London.

1871   The Paris Commune. *The Civil War in France.* Conference of the International in London.

1872   Last Congress of the International at The Hague. Expulsion of Bakunin.

1875   Unification congress of the German workers' parties at Gotha. Founding of the Social Democratic party of Germany. *Critique of the Gotha Programme.*

1878   The Social Democratic party banned in Germany.

1881   Death of Jenny Marx on December 2.

1883   Death of Karl Marx on March 14.

1885   *Capital*, Volume II, edited by Engels.

1894   *Capital*, Volume III, edited by Engels.

AUTHOR'S FOREWORD

To select what is essential from the vast body of Karl Marx's work—philosophy, political economy, anthropology, social criticism, history, theory of revolutionary practice, visions of the future—and to comment on these essentials, all in the space of barely two hundred pages, under the ambitious title of *Marx in His Own Words*, is a bold undertaking indeed. My friend Franz Marek and I, working in collaboration, have attempted to carry it out. Marx *really said* every word of the texts we quote: but, should anyone point out that he said a great deal more besides, we should be the first to agree. He did say a great deal more, and he made great demands upon his readers. With the exception of a few texts he is not an easy author to read. My collaborator and I were faced over and over again with the question: how much may we expect from our readers without making them lose heart? How much may we simplify without injury to Marx's greatness and originality? We have presupposed an intelligent reader—yourself—and we have endeavored, for your information, to put the real Marx against the distorted image so often presented of him.

Marx the revolutionary thinker, Marx the man was far from being an infallible Father of any Church, a cold analyst, or an advocate of violence.

Filled to the brim with the "principle of greatness," he combined vision with science, philosophy with practice, theory with action—passionately, radically, intolerantly: a man who set out not merely to interpret the world but to change it, and whose ideas have gripped millions of human beings and are still shaking the world.

35

We have chosen to let Marx speak for himself. Our comments are confined to pointing out certain connections, rendering comprehension easier, separating what is permanent from what was time-conditioned and has been overtaken by historical development—that is to say, applying the critical method of Marxism to Marxism itself.

The reader we visualize has an open mind. He has had enough of propaganda of every kind, and wishes only to be informed.

1

THE DREAM OF
THE WHOLE MAN

Marx's entire lifework was motivated by "the dream of a whole man," of an integrated human being—the basis of an integrated humanity—in which the humanity that resides within each individual would be realized. The realization of this inner potential of human beings, which for Marx was the same as the development of human freedom, required the transcendence of the alienation of human beings from each other and themselves. It required the liberation of humanity from the pursuit of narrow economic ends and the opening up of wider realms of creativity. This humanism in Marx's vision, Fischer demonstrates, was apparent in both Marx's treatment of religion and in his dialectical method.—*JBF*

Marx's thought underwent many variations in the course of his life, but what had served as his starting point remained intact: the possibility of the whole, the *total* man.

Since the triumph of the industrial revolution and of the capitalist method of production at the turn of the eighteenth century, the fragmentation of man through the division of labor, mechanization, exploitation, and commerce had become the fundamental European experience. The longing for unity with one's own self, with one's kind, and with nature, from which man had become alienated, was common to all those who entertained humanist feelings and ideas.

In their romantic revolt against a world which turned everything into a commodity and degraded man to the status of an object, the poets and philosophers of the iron age complained that man had become a fragment of his own self, had been overpowered by his own works, had fallen away from himself.

Enjoyment was divorced from labor, the means from the end, the effort from the reward. Everlastingly chained to a single little fragment of the Whole, man himself develops into nothing but a fragment; everlastingly in his ear the monotonous sound of the wheel that he turns, he never develops the harmony of his being, and instead of putting the stamp of humanity upon his own nature, he becomes nothing more than the imprint of his occupation or of his specialized knowledge. (Friedrich Schiller, *On the Aesthetic Education of Man, in a Series of Letters*, trans., Elizabeth M. Wilkinson and L.A. Willoughby [Oxford, 1967: Clarendon Press], sixth letter, p. 35.)

The age of turbulent development of technology and industry, of greed and the mercantile spirit, of capital and of proletarian misery, of revolutionary hopes and their disappointment by post-revolutionary reality, became the age of romantic protest against the complacent bourgeoisie. Both the aristocratic and the plebeian opponents of the bourgeois world joined in that protest; both condemned the dehumanization of man by the progressive division of labor whose extreme consequence, at one end of society, was ever-increasing wealth and, at the other, ever-increasing material and spiritual wretchedness. But, as time went on, a certain differentiation took place within the romantic movement: some looked to the past as the only mainspring of salvation and imagined it as a time of human unity and dignity; others turned towards the future, dreaming of the resurgence of the whole man in a coming realm of freedom, abundance, and humanity.

The political revolution in America and France had proclaimed man's right to liberty—the "free personality." The contrast between such proclamations and the reality which followed was painful to many. Man in bourgeois society had indeed become an individual—not in community with others, but in harsh competition against them. "Liberty as a right of man," wrote the young Marx, "is not founded upon the relations between man and man, but rather upon the separation of man from man."[1]

None of the supposed rights of man, therefore, go beyond the egoistic man, man as he is, as a member of civil society; that is, an individual separated from the community, withdrawn into himself, wholly preoccupied with his private interest and acting in accordance with his private caprice.[2]

The problem therefore was to turn men, reduced to an empty individuality, away from purely private interests and preoccupations, to unite the individual with a community based on the freedom of all rather than on the dominance of a few.

The notes Marx made for his doctoral thesis at Berlin University at the age of twenty-one do not as yet contain any mention of the class struggle, of the proletariat and revolution, of the "realm of freedom" in a classless society without rulers. But we do find, in the sixth notebook, the following sentence on the subjectivism, the fundamental self-centeredness of the epicurean and stoical philosophies: "Thus, when the universal sun has set, does the moth seek the lamp-light of privacy!" And even earlier, in the third notebook: "He who no longer finds pleasure in building the whole world with his own forces, in being a world-creator instead of revolving forever inside his own skin, on him the Spirit has spoken its anathema." And finally, in the seventh notebook: "Least of all are we entitled to assume, on the strength of authority and good faith, that a philosophy is a philosophy, even if the authority is that of a whole nation and the faith is that of centuries."[3]

The "universal sun" for Marx was the individual's commitment to a common goal, his participation in the *res publica*, the public cause, the fact that his actions and ideas could transcend narrow private interest—in other words, something like Athenian democracy or the Roman republic before the dictatorship of the Caesars. Marx refused to "revolve forever inside his own skin": he wanted to be a "world-creator," making the world intellectually his own and eventually contributing to its material transformation. The desire for a new social dawn, for a "universal" sun that would make the lamplight of privacy appear dull by comparison, is unmistakable. But equally there is the stirring of a critical mind unprepared to accept authority and good faith as proof of the truth of any philosophy, doctrine, or system. Marx at twenty-one was already eager to forge ahead towards a new universality, to be the creator of a new world—without forgoing the right to submit everything already in existence, or coming into existence, to critical re-examination.

In Berlin, where Marx read jurisprudence, philosophy, and history, the dominant spirit was that of Hegel, who exercised a great fascination over the younger scholars and thinkers. In his gigantic philosophical opus, which was both the crowning point and the negation of romanticism, Hegel saw the world spirit in world history traverse every successive form of alienation—of the falling away from the self—and simultaneously also of the return to the self, of reconciliation, thus progressing from an unconscious unity with the self to a conscious one. Hegel's difficult philosophy was a manifestation of the contradictory dynamic of his age—the notion of development, the dream of a realm of freedom and plenitude, of a reality that has become conscious of itself.

Marx as a young man at first rejected Hegel, but was soon captivated by the great philosopher and his dialectic. He was to remain faithful to the dialectic—the inner contradiction within the nature of thought and of all things, the recognition that nothing can be understood in isolation or as a rectilinear sequence of cause and effect, but only as the multiple interaction of all factors and as being in conflict with itself: that everything, as it comes into being, produces its own negation and tends to progress towards the negation of the negation. But he went far beyond Hegel in the consequences he drew.

As editor of the liberal *Rheinische Zeitung* in 1842 to 1843, Marx with his radical-democratic views became a thorn in the flesh of the Germany of the 1840s and had to move to Paris. Writing in the *Deutsch-Französische Jahrbücher* in 1844, he described and castigated the conditions in Germany from which he had escaped in the following words:

> German history, indeed, prides itself upon a development which no other nation had previously accomplished, or will ever imitate in the historical sphere. We have shared in the restorations of modern nations without ever sharing in their revolutions. We have been restored, first because other nations have dared to make revolutions, and secondly because other nations have suffered counter-revolutions; in the first case because our masters were afraid, and in the second case because they were not afraid. Led by our shepherds, we have only once kept company with liberty and that was on the day of its interment.[4]

In Paris Marx met the young Frederick Engels, the son of a manufacturer from the Rhineland, then working in London. Through him he not only gained an insight into the social conditions prevailing in the most advanced industrial country of the time, but, above all, Engels became a friend such as there have been only few in history. During the collaboration which followed and which was unparalleled in its closeness and in the length of its duration, Engels recognized—without a trace of envy—the surpassing genius of his occasionally somewhat difficult friend, and became his devoted helper not only in intellectual, scientific, and political matters but also, over and over again, in private life. Engels's philosophical contribution to Marxism can be contested: but the productive and enduring friendship which united Marx and Engels stands high above all criticism.

What Marx came to know in Paris was the proletariat.

He saw the wretched figure of the proletarian as the quintessence of dehumanization, the extreme of everything the Romantics felt to be the denial and mockery of the nature of man. But precisely in this extreme negation Marx saw the hope of overcoming it. He believed that the proletariat was forced by its very poverty to liberate itself from inhuman conditions by overturning those conditions at their base, and that, by liberating itself, it would become the liberator of mankind.

There is an extraordinary poignancy about the way Marx described the negation of man as found in the proletarian of his time.

> Labor certainly produces marvels for the rich, but it produces privation for the worker. It produces palaces, but hovels for the worker. It produces beauty, but deformity for the worker. It replaces labor by machinery, but it casts some of the workers back into a barbarous kind of work and turns the others into machines. It produces intelligence, but also stupidity and cretinism for the workers.[5]

The proletarian in his work does not fulfil himself but denies himself,

> has a feeling of misery rather than well-being, does not develop freely his mental and physical energies but is physically exhausted and mentally debased. The worker therefore feels himself at home only during his leisure time, whereas at work he feels homeless.[6]

Marx was, of course, a master of needle-sharp comment, but many contemporary records prove that he was not exaggerating when he spoke of the wretchedness of the proletarian. The Young Hegelians, the great philosopher's radical disciples, expected atheism to liberate man by bringing his spirit back from the beyond into the real world. Marx's view was more profound; the criticism of religion was for him "the premise of all criticism," but he was aware of the need for liberation from material as well as spiritual bondage, and he saw religion both as "the expression of real misery" and as the "protest against real misery." "Religion is the sigh of the oppressed creature, the sentiment of a heartless world, and the soul of soulless conditions. It is the *opium* of the people."[7] As is so often the case, not many people are aware of what Marx really said in this context: the quotation is usually twisted to imply that religion was opium for the people, that is to say a narcotic given the people by outside forces, while the preceding sentence is ignored.

> *Atheism*, as a denial of this unreality [the unreality of man and nature], is no longer meaningful, for atheism is a *negation of God* and seeks to assert by this negation the *existence of man*. Socialism no longer requires such a roundabout method; it begins from the *theoretical* and *practical sense perception* of man and nature as essential beings. It is positive human *self-consciousness*, no longer a self-consciousness attained through the negation of religion; just as the *real life* of man is positive and no longer attained through the negation of private property, through communism.... Communism is the necessary form and the dynamic principle of the immediate future, but communism is not itself the goal of human development, the form of human society.[8]

We can see that religion, atheism, and communism were, for Marx, stages or features of development rather than its goal. The goal was positive humanism, the real life of man. The existence of the proletariat was the most striking contradiction of such a life; but "the ruptured reality of industry" did not manifest itself in the proletariat alone. Scientific analysis of capitalist industry confirmed a hundred times over what Schiller had only apprehended: that "enjoyment was divorced from labor, the means from the end, the effort from the reward"; that the proletarian was only the most extreme expression of the fragmentary, disconnected, rent nature of the world of machines, profits, and poverty. As the negation became more clearly pronounced, so the thing it negated became clearer too: the unrealized image of man.

The starting point of religion is God. Hegel's starting point was the State. Marx's was Man.

In the *Critique of Hegel's State Law* Marx wrote:

> Hegel proceeds from the State and makes man the State subjectified; democracy proceeds from man and makes the State man objectified....

> Man does not exist for law's sake, law exists for man's sake; it is *human existence*, whereas [for] the others man is *legal existence*. That is the fundamental difference of democracy.[9]

The decisive thing for Marx is not simply "the universal," a system as an end in itself, but man—concrete, real, individual man. The object of his thinking, of all his efforts, is the whole man, the reality of man, positive humanism.

Man needs the community in order to develop into a free individual. "In the previous substitutes for the community, in the State, etc., personal freedom has existed only for the individuals who developed within the relationships of this ruling class, and only in so far as they were individuals of the class." Individuals who behave as though they were independent are in actual fact conditioned not only by the whole of social development—by language, tradition, upbringing, etc.—but also by their class, estate, or profession. Their personality is conditioned and determined by quite definite class relationships. Although the mutual relationship between them is a relationship between persons, it is above all one between "social character masks"—not as specific individuals, but as standardized "average individuals." Marx hoped and believed that with the "community of revolutionary proletarians" it would be just the reverse: individuals would participate in it as individuals. Marx saw communism, and, with it, common control over the conditions which "were previously abandoned to chance and had won an independent existence over against the separate individuals just because of their separation as individuals,"[10] not as a system of classes and castes—of "social character masks"—but as a free association of individual men.

Between the individual and society there is an interaction:

> As society itself produces *man* as *man*, so it is *produced* by him.... The *human* significance of nature only exists for *social* man, because only in this case is nature a *bond* with other men, the basis of his existence for others and of their existence for him. Only then is nature the *basis* of his own *human* experience and a vital element of human reality.[11]

Although our time of scientific and technical revolution calls for an ever-increasing measure of teamwork, the work of a scholar, a writer, or an artist is not *directly* bound up with other people and may actually suffer from direct social intervention. Yet such work presupposes a community with others; it draws on the experience of others, it is essentially a form of social activity despite all its autonomy.

It is not only the material of my activity—such as the language itself which the thinker uses—which is given to me as a social product. My *own existence* is a social activity. For this reason, what I myself produce I produce for society, and with the consciousness of acting as a social being.[12]

This is not flat utilitarianism, not just a matter of one's activity being of direct use to society. The point here is the social nature of the individual—*the personality as the outcome and justification of society.*

> Though man is a unique individual—and it is just his particularity which makes him an individual, a really *individual* communal being—he is equally the *whole*, the ideal whole, the subjective existence of society as thought and experienced. He exists in reality as the representation and the real mind of social existence, and as the sum of human manifestations of life.[13]

This totality of man proclaimed by Marx, this "humanity in man's nature" as Schiller called it, is at first only an idea, only (but for a few exceptions) a possibility as yet unrealized. Fragmentary, imperfect, disfigured man is incapable of transforming himself into total man; he can only do so through society as it develops. The more a man is able to take possession of the outside world—through his senses, his spirit, his intelligence—and the more integrated and many-sided this taking of possession, this "appropriation" is, the greater is his chance of becoming a *whole* man.

> Man appropriates his manifold being in an all-inclusive way, and thus as a whole man. All his *human* relations to the world—seeing, hearing, smelling, tasting, touching, thinking, observing, feeling, desiring, acting, loving—in short, all the organs of his individuality, like the organs which are directly communal in form, are in their objective action (their *action in relation to the object*) an appropriation of this object, the appropriation of human reality. The way in which they react to the object is the confirmation of *human reality*. It is human effectiveness and human suffering, for suffering humanly considered is an enjoyment of the self for man.[14]

The objects which man makes his own through his senses, his intellect and his imagination become his own objectification: he unites with them, makes them his own creation and part of his own self by absorbing them. The whole development of the human race is needed in order to humanize the senses and to educate them so that they became *human* senses.

Many commentators overlooked the fact that when Marx speaks of this "all-inclusive" appropriation and of the "man endowed with all the senses," he in fact means a creative act, an artistic act in the broadest sense of that term: that, for

Marx, love was an essential form of such "appropriation." In a world of possession, of commerce and profit, this humane act has shriveled into the mere act of *having*. Marx speaks with passion against the mentality of *having*, which sees immediate, physical possession as "the unique goal of life and existence."[15] This mentality has infected love itself, twisting the relationship between man and woman into a relationship of ownership and domination; marriage in its present form— "a form of exclusive private property"—and the demand of a "crude and unreflective communism" for the common owner- ship of women are both concerned with *appropriation through having* and therefore mean man's debasement and reduction to a *thing*.

> In the relationship with *woman*, as the prey and the handmaid of communal lust, is expressed the infinite degradation in which man exists for himself.... From this relationship man's whole level of development can be assessed. It follows from the character of this relationship how far *man* has become, and has understood himself as, a *species-being*, a *human* being. The relationship of man to woman is the *most natural* relation of human being to human being. It indicates, therefore, how far man's natural behavior has become *human*, and how far his *human* essence has become a *natural* essence for him, how far his *human nature* has become *nature* for him. It also shows how far man's needs have become *human* needs, and conse- quently how far the other person, as a person, has become one of his needs, and to what extent he is in his individual existence at the same time a social being.[16]

The most natural relationship thus becomes a measure of humanization: the development from faceless sexuality to "higher sexual union" (as Goethe called it), a community of the senses, the spirit, and the mind, a recognition of the other as a fellow being, does not destroy nature but enhances it until it becomes true *human nature*. In 1843 Marx married a beautiful bride, Jenny von Westphalen. On June 21, 1856 he wrote his wife a letter from London in which he said:

> Momentary absence is good, for present things appear too alike for us to distinguish them. Even towers when they are close seem dwarfish, whereas small everyday things, when they are close, loom far too large. Small habits which assume the form of passions when they are close to us, disappear as soon as their immediate object is out of sight. Great passions which, because of the proximity of their object, take on the form of small habits, grow and reassume their natural dimensions by the magic effect of distance. Thus it is with my love. You only need to be removed from me—if only by dreams—

and I know at once that time does to my love for you what sun and rain do to a plant: it makes it grow. My love for you, as soon as you are far away, appears as what it is, a giant wherein all the energy of my mind and all the character of my heart is concentrated. I feel a man once more because I feel a great passion. The complexities in which study and modern education involve us, the skepticism we must necessarily bring to bear on all subjective and objective impressions, are perfectly designed to make all of us small and weak and petulant and undecided. But love, not the love of Feuerbach's Man nor Moleschott's metabolism, nor again love of the Proletariat, but love of the beloved and more particularly of you, makes a man a man again....

"Buried in her arms, revived by her kisses"—yes, in your arms and by your kisses—and the Brahmins and Pythagoras can keep their doctrine of reincarnation for all I care, and Christianity its teaching of the Resurrection.[17]

Thus, by appropriation through love, nature has become human nature.

Man educates himself to be a man by humanizing his nature, by refusing to degrade other men into objects but, instead, by making the objects of nature his own—humanly apprehended, recognized, formed objects by means of whose human appropriation he develops the wealth of his capabilities and the plenitude of his own self. Appropriation by having, fragmentation of potential plenitude into a patchwork of private property, makes man "stupid and partial." Yet appropriation by possession has been and still is the inevitable step towards a fully productive society in which demands grow in step with capacities and man is not degraded to an object—in other words, a truly human society.

Marx was not a lachrymose moral preacher. While revealing the monstrous nature of appropriation through having, of the rule of private ownership and the dehumanization of man through the capitalist method of production he recognized it to be a necessary phase of historical development and saw a new reality ripening within it.

Private property has made us so stupid and partial that an object is only *ours* when we have it, when it exists for us as capital or when it is directly eaten, drunk, worn, inhabited, etc., in short *utilized* in some way....

Thus *all* the physical and intellectual senses have been replaced by the simple alienation of *all* these senses; the sense of *having*. The human being had to be reduced to this absolute poverty in order to be able to give birth to all his inner wealth.[18]

A sense that is cramped by crude practical necessity is bound to be a sadly limited one. To a starving man, it matters little whether food is presented in a form fit for human consumption or not: he cares only for its abstract existence as food. "It could just as well exist in the most crude form, and it is impossible to say in what this feeding-activity would differ from that of animals."[19]

What does this mean? It means that there must be no more starving people, that society must not only become capable of satisfying the most primitive requirements but must advance towards higher, more differentiated needs—needs which are no longer animal but human. The material for such a future is accumulated in the society of private ownership.

> Just as society at its beginnings finds, through the development of *private property* with its wealth and poverty (both intellectual and material), the materials necessary for this *cultural development,* so fully constituted society produces man in all the plenitude of his being, the wealthy man endowed with all the senses, as an enduring reality.[20]

Marx saw bourgeois society with all its contradictions as a society *in the process of becoming.* He dreamed of communism as a society that had completed this process. He did not expect communism to be the simple negation of private property but its positive abolition in a world of plenty, of humanity and integrated intelligence: "the real appropriation of human nature through and for man."[21]

Communism as Marx anticipated it was "the *definitive* resolution of the antagonism between man and nature, and between man and man." He hoped that communism would mean the transformation of "naturalism" (that is to say the premises supplied by nature) into "humanism" (that is to say the full flowering of total, conscious, and no longer divided man). Both in his youth and at the end of his life Marx's aim was not the deadening but the humanizing of the senses; not the replacement of the body by the mind or vice versa but the development of all capacities for production or enjoyment; not material or spiritual impoverishment but all-round appropriation of the world and all its possibilities; not standardization and depersonalization but the manifold nature of individuality living in a free community with others.

Did Marx, then, see communism as a final state, an elysium, a paradise? On the contrary: for him it meant the mere

beginning of true human development. Dreams always precede reality. Thought precedes action.

> In order to supersede the *idea* of private property communist *ideas*
> are sufficient, but genuine communist activity is necessary in
> order to supersede *real* private property. History will produce it,
> and the development which we already recognize in thought as
> self-transcending will in reality involve a severe and protracted
> process. We must consider it an advance, however, that we have
> previously acquired an awareness of the limited nature and the
> goal of the historical development and can see beyond it.[22]

Consciousness, then, goes farther than the goal and farther
than the limitations of historical progress; it does not see
communism as a final state but only as a phase in a development which, in principle, has no end; but it has the courage
to believe in a utopia.

In later years Marx saw that radiant far-off vision of a utopia
in less vivid colors, but he never abandoned it. To the very
end of his life he remained convinced that the positive abolition of private ownership of the means of production, the
scientific nature of labor, the substitution of machines for men
would bring *the whole man* into being and enable him to
unfold the full range of his potential abilities.

Marx (and Engels even more) at first believed that the whole
man would be formed within the sphere of socially necessary,
useful production by mastering machines and constantly
changing the nature of his activity. But Marx later abandoned
this notion. As early as 1857-1858, in the draft entitled
Grundrisse der Kritik der Politischen Ökonomie (*Foundations
of the Critique of Political Economy*), he laid stress on the
"artistic scientific education of individuals as a result of time
becoming free for everyone," but thought it possible that the
"immediate material process of production" might be divested of
its form as "necessity."[23]

In his last work, the third volume of *Capital*, he revised this
view.

> The actual wealth of society, and the possibility of constantly expand-
> ing its reproduction process, therefore, do not depend upon the
> duration of surplus-labor, but upon its productivity and the more or
> less copious conditions of production under which it is performed.
> In fact, the realm of freedom actually begins only where labor which
> is determined by necessity and mundane considerations ceases; thus
> in the very nature of things it lies beyond the sphere of actual material
> production. Just as the savage must wrestle with Nature to satisfy

his wants, to maintain and reproduce life, so must civilized man, and he must do so in all social formations and under all possible modes of production. With his development this realm of physical necessity expands as a result of his wants; but, at the same time, the forces of production which satisfy these wants also increase. Freedom in this field can only consist in socialized man, the associated producers, rationally regulating their interchange with Nature, bringing it under their common control, instead of being ruled by it as the blind forces of Nature; and achieving this with the least expenditure of energy and under conditions most favorable to, and worthy of, their human nature. But it nonetheless remains a realm of necessity. Beyond it begins that development of human energy which is an end in itself, the true realm of freedom, which, however, can blossom forth only with this realm of necessity as its basis. The shortening of the working-day is its basic prerequisite.[24]

The "realm of freedom" beyond the narrow sphere of material production as the true realm of man, of man's flowering in the midst of science and art, love and serenity, community and personal freedom—this greatest of all utopias is outlined in the work of the young Marx and remains preserved in the works of his maturity and old age. For Marx, the quintessence of positive humanism was not "abstract," monotonous labor which reduces man to a fragment of himself, but creative work, the development of the human potential which is its own goal.

2

CREATIVE LABOR

Marx defined human beings as creative beings, able to transform their relation to nature and to each other. Labor—understood in its broadest sense as the realm of human creativity and productive activity—is what distinguishes the human species from all other species. Only humanity is capable of self-creation based on conscious activity. It is this view of humanity as *homo faber* (the maker) which underlies Marx's entire analysis of historical development.—*JBF*

For Marx, the outstanding achievement of Hegel's philosophy was above all "that Hegel grasps the self-creation of man as a process ... that he, therefore, grasps the nature of *labor*, and conceives objective man (true, because real man) as the result of his *own labor*."[25] [...]

"In short, Hegel conceives labor as man's *act of self-creation* (though in abstract terms) ... as the demonstration of his alien being."[26]

The animal is one with its life activity. It does not distinguish the aim itself. It is *its activity*. But man makes his life activity itself an object of his will and consciousness. He has a conscious life activity....

The practical construction of an *objective world*, the *manipulation* of inorganic nature, is the confirmation of man as a conscious species-being, i.e. a being who treats the species as his own being or himself as a species-being. Of course, animals also produce. They construct nests, dwellings, as in the case of bees, beavers, ants, etc. But they only produce what is strictly necessary for themselves or their young. They produce only in a single direction, while man produces universally. They produce only under the compulsion of direct physical need, while man produces when he is free from physical need and only truly produces in freedom from such need. Animals produce only themselves, while man reproduces the whole of nature. The products of animal production belong directly to their physical bodies, while man is free in face of his product...

It is just in his work upon the objective world that man really proves himself as a *species-being*. This production is his active species-life.

By means of it nature appears as *his* work and his reality. The object of labor is, therefore, the *objectification of man's species-life*; for he no longer reproduces himself merely intellectually, as in consciousness, but actively and in a real sense, and he sees his own reflection in a world which he has constructed.[27]

Man as the creator of himself, as the product, capable of development and change, of his own labor, as a living being objectifying himself in his work and confronting himself in the reality he has created: that is the central theme of the philosophy Marx found already existing in rough outline when he grew up. He was to enrich it by a number of essential insights and to draw the consequences it implied. The striking thing about the *Economic and Philosophical Manuscripts*—which, after all, were only a draft—is the manner in which the philosophical principle of labor is interlinked with the historical manifestations of labor. The fact that man "only truly produces in freedom from physical need" is the anticipation of a state not yet achieved, or only sporadically achieved in history. But to perceive this creative nature of labor at its very origin was to discover the inexhaustible possibilities hidden in man as a working being.

This living being had emerged from nature in the darkness of time, representing nature and anti-nature at the same time, different from all other species by *conscious activity*. Marx was fully aware that many conditions must have combined to make this emergence possible, but he refused to become involved in biological or any other speculations based on fantasy rather than on science. What mattered to him was the new *quality* regardless of the processes which had created it: the essence of the new species: labor.

The species-nature of animals is an eternal repetition, that of man is transformation, development, change. An animal is the past incarnate in the present; man is not only past and present, but also the future. An animal accepts what nature offers; man forces nature to give him more. He lays hands on nature, enters into conflict with it, alienates himself from it and takes possession of what has become alien by making it serve his purpose—by *working* it.

Man *works himself out* of nature, forming his man-nature by his hands, his consciousness, and his imagination in community with other men.

What, then, is labor—apparently so easy to define, but in reality open to so many definitions and in its effects so infinite?

> Labor is, in the first place, a process in which both man and Nature participate, and in which man of his own accord starts, regulates, and controls the material reactions between himself and Nature. He opposes himself to Nature as one of her own forces, setting in motion arms and legs, head and hands, the natural forces of his body, in order to appropriate Nature's productions in a form adapted to his own wants. By thus acting on the external world and changing it, he at the same time changes his own nature. He develops his slumbering powers and compels them to act in obedience to his sway. We are not now dealing with those primitive instinctive forms of labor that remind us of the mere animal. An immeasurable interval of time separates the state of things in which a man brings his labor-power to market for sale as a commodity, from that state in which human labor was still in its first instinctive stage. We presuppose labor in a form that stamps it as exclusively human. A spider conducts operations that resemble those of a weaver, and a bee puts to shame many an architect in the construction of her cells. But what distinguishes the worst architect from the best of bees is this, that the architect raises his structure in imagination before he erects it in reality. At the end of every labor-process, we get a result that already existed in the imagination of the laborer at its commencements.[28]

In order to determine the nature of labor Marx presupposes it in an already developed form and takes account of the fact that it has a long history. Labor begins with the utilization of an "occasional tool" found in nature and proceeds to the discovery that such tools can be reproduced and given a more efficient form. In other words, the means to achieve a purpose precedes the worker's sense of purpose, the ideal result anticipated in his imagination. Marx hints that labor must not be merely effort, not only a curse upon mankind condemned to labor by the sweat of its brow, but that it must carry the worker along as the "play" of his own physical and spiritual forces, and thus unite the performance principle with the pleasure principle. In a polemic against Adam Smith, Marx opposed the *creative* principle inherent in labor to the "historical forms of labor as slave, *corvée* or wage labor." In these historical forms labor is *external compulsion* and has lost its purpose "as self-realization, objectification of the subject, hence as the real freedom which its action constitutes."[29]

The instinctive form of early labor was transcended by *instruments of labor*.

The use and fabrication of instruments of labor, although existing in the germ among certain species of animals, is specifically characteristic of the human labor-process, and Franklin therefore defines man as a tool-making animal. Relics of bygone instruments of labor possess the same importance for the investigation of extinct economic forms of society, as do fossil bones for the determination of extinct species of animals. It is not the articles made, but how they are made, and by what instruments, that enables us to distinguish different economic epochs. Instruments of labor not only supply a standard of the degree of development to which human labor has attained, but they are also indicators of the social conditions under which that labor is carried on....

In the labor-process, therefore, man's activity, with the help of the instruments of labor, effects an alteration, designed from the commencement, in the material worked upon. The process disappears in the product; the latter is a use-value, Nature's material adapted by a change of form to the wants of man. Labor has incorporated itself with its subject: the former is materialized, the latter transformed. That which in the laborer appeared as movement, now appears in the product as a fixed quality without motion.[30]

The interaction established by labor between man and natural substance manifests itself in the dual nature of labor as production and consumption:

Labor uses up its material factors, its subject and its instruments, consumes them, and is therefore a process of consumption. Such productive consumption is distinguished from individual consumption by this, that the latter uses up products, as means of subsistence for the living individual; the former, as means whereby alone, labor, the labor-power of the living individual, is enabled to act.[31]

But it is not only a question of labor consuming the natural substance: the natural substance also consumes the energy of the worker. When labor is creative, this energy is returned to the worker, not only as the work product—as humanized natural substance—but also as confirmation of his individuality and his latent potential.

The labor-process, resolved as above into its simple elementary factors, is human action with a view to the production of use-values, appropriation of natural substances to human requirements; it is the necessary condition for effecting exchange of matter between man and Nature; it is the everlasting Nature-imposed condition of human existence, and therefore is independent of every social phase of that existence, or rather, is common to every such phase.[32]

Before we turn to the historical forms of labor determined by the development of instruments of labor, by the increasing division of labor, by production of commodities for the market, by *having* and *ruling*, let us emphasize once more how much importance Marx always attached to the *principle of labor as man's species-nature.* To see labor as the anticipation of the work product is to see man as a being that projects, plans, and constructs the future. The first tool contains within it all the potential future ones. The first recognition of the fact that the world can be changed by conscious activity contains all future, as yet unknown, but inevitable change. A living being which has once begun to make nature his own through the work of his hands, his intellect, and his imagination, will never stop. Every achievement opens the door to unconquered territory.

But when labor is destructive, not creative, when it is undertaken under coercion and not as the free play of forces, when it means the withering, not the flowering, of man's physical and intellectual potential, then labor is a denial of its own principle and therefore of the principle of man.

3

DIVISION OF LABOR AND ALIENATION

Some interpreters of Marx have argued that his concept of alienation was a product of his earliest phase as a student of Hegelian philosophy, before his emergence as a mature thinker in his own right (beginning with the publication of the *Theses on Feuerbach* in 1846; see Appendix). In this chapter, Fischer explains how this analysis of alienation actually pervades Marx's work from beginning to end. Marx's concept of alienation, of the creative potential of human labor under class society, actually deepened over the years, as his understanding of the crippling effects of the detailed division of labor under capitalism developed. His critique of the alienating conditions imposed by private property was at the heart of his conception of the need for a transcendence of present-day social conditions. Throughout his life, Marx adhered to the view that, as Fischer put it, "material life is the basis but not the purpose of human existence."—*JBF*

In principle, labor is conceived as a *whole,* as man's species-nature, the collective creative activity of mankind. But if its possibilities are to be properly exploited and the full potential latent in mankind is to be activated, labor must become a *multiple* activity divided into many separate ones; for no individual and no community limited in place and time is capable of doing what mankind as a whole is called upon to do. In order, then, to become all-embracing, labor evolved a multitude of one-sided activities; in order to expand production, it was necessary to narrow down individual work processes, and in order to make possible a state of universal wealth—a plenitude of material and spiritual goods—*the enrichment of the few* and *poverty for the majority* were unavoidable for thousands of years.

The division of labor not only destroyed unity: by introducing inequality among the various occupations, it created and reinforced social inequality. Labor was not, and still is not,

55

divided up into equal parts, but is divided for the profit of the stronger and the disadvantage of the weaker.

Marx distinguishes between the *social* division of labor and the division of labor *in manufacture*, that is to say within society and within each work process. These two categories overlap and interlink continually.

> If we keep labor alone in view, we may designate the separation of social production into its main division or *genera*—viz., agriculture, industries, etc.—as division of labor in general, and the splitting up of these families into species and sub-species, as division of labor in particular, and the division of labor within the workshop as division of labor in singular or in detail.[33]

The division of social production into its broad categories leads to the creation of private property and splits society up into haves and have-nots, rulers and ruled, exploiters and exploited.

> Division of labor in a society, and the corresponding tying down of individuals to a particular calling, develops itself, just as does the division of labor in manufacture, from opposite starting points. Within a family and after further development within a tribe,* there springs up naturally a division of labor, caused by differences of sex and age, a division that is consequently based on a purely physiological foundation, which division enlarges its materials by the expansion of the community by the increase of population, and more especially, by the conflicts between different tribes, and the subjugation of one tribe by another.[34]

Marx drew attention repeatedly to the importance of conquest—territorial occupation—for social division of labor and the emergence of private property. We quote one such passage.

> *War* is among the original labors of each of these primitive communities, both for the maintenance of property and for its acquisition.... If man is conquered along with land as being its organic accessory, he is conquered as one of the conditions of production, and this gives rise to slavery and serfdom, which soon falsify and change the original form of any community and become the basis for a new form.[35]

---

* In the *Grundrisse*, a text that represents his preliminary work on *Capital*, Marx assumed the tribe—rather than the family—to be the original social unit. Subsequent scientific discoveries have confirmed this assumption.

On the other hand ... the exchange of products springs up at the points where different families, tribes, communities, come in contact; for, in the beginning of civilization, it is not private individuals but families, tribes, etc., that meet on an independent footing. Different communities find different means of production and different means of subsistence in their natural environment. Hence, their modes of production and of living, and their products, are different. It is this spontaneously developed difference which, when different communities come in contact, calls forth the mutual exchange of products, and the consequent gradual conversion of those products into commodities.... The so-called division of labor arises from the exchange between spheres of production, that are originally distinct and independent of one another.[36]

Increasing population and production, power and commerce are, therefore, the necessary pre-conditions for the division of labor.

The greatest division of material and mental labor is the separation of town and country. The antagonism between town and country begins with the transition from barbarism to civilization, from tribe to State, from locality to nation, and runs through the whole history of civilization to the present day.... The existence of the town implies, at the same time, the necessity of administration, police, taxes, etc., in short, of the municipality, and thus of politics in general. Here first became manifest the division of the population into two great classes, which is directly based on the division of labor and on the instruments of production. The town already is in actual fact the concentration of the population, of the instruments of production, of capital, of pleasures, of needs, while the country demonstrates just the opposite fact, their isolation and separation. The antagonism of town and country can only exist as a result of private property. It is the most crass expression of the subjection of the individual under the division of labor, under a definite activity forced upon him—a subjection which makes one man into a restricted town-animal, the other into a restricted country-animal, and daily creates anew the conflict between their interests.[37]

The division of labor, both socially and in manufacture, entails not only the development and objectification of the potential gifts latent in the human race, but also "a certain mental and physical crippling."[38]

The craftsman was still at home with himself, producing something rounded and complete, for all its limitations.

In the towns, the division of labor between the individual guilds was as yet quite natural, and, in the guilds themselves, not at all developed between the individual workers. Every workman had to be versed in a whole round of tasks, had to be able to make everything that was to be made with his tools. The limited commerce and the scanty communication between the individual towns, the lack of population and the narrow needs did not allow of a higher division of labor, and therefore every man who wished to become a master had to be proficient in the whole of his craft. Thus there is found with medieval craftsmen an interest in their special work and a proficiency in it, which was capable of rising to a narrow artistic sense. For this very reason, however, every medieval craftsman was completely absorbed in his work, to which he had a contented, slavish relationship, and to which he was subjected to a far greater extent than the modern worker whose work is a matter of indifference to him.[39]

The personal relationship of the craftsman to his product first began to change with the manufacturing systems, in which division of labor began to predominate. But the later introduction of machinery led to a radical depersonalization of the worker.

In the first place, in the form of machinery, the implements of labor become automatic, things moving and working independent of the workman. They are thenceforth an industrial *perpetuum mobile* that would go on producing forever, did it not meet with certain natural obstructions in the weak bodies and the strong wills of its human attendants.[40]

Along with the tool, the skill of the workman in handling it passes over to the machine. The capabilities of the tool are emancipated from the restraints that are inseparable from human labor-power. Thereby the technical foundation on which is based the division of labor in Manufacture, is swept away. Hence, in the place of the hierarchy of specialized workmen that characterizes manufacture, there steps, in the automatic factory, a tendency to equalize and reduce to one and the same level every kind of work that has to be done by the minders of the machines, in the place of the artificially produced differentiations of the detail workmen, step the natural differences of age and sex.[41]

In handicrafts and manufacture, the workman makes use of a tool, in the factory, the machine makes use of him. There the movements of the instrument of labor proceed from him, here it is the movements of the machine that he must follow. In manufacture the workmen are parts of a living mechanism. In the factory we have a lifeless mechanism independent of the workman, who becomes its mere living appendage....

At the same time that factory work exhausts the nervous system to the uttermost, it does away with the many-sided play of the muscles, and confiscates every atom of freedom, both in bodily and intellectual activity. The lightening of the labor, even, becomes a sort of torture, since the machine does not free the laborer from work, but deprives the work of all interest... The special skill of each individual insignificant factory operative vanishes as an infinitesimal quantity before the science, the gigantic physical forces, and the mass of labor that are embodied in the factory mechanism and, together with that mechanism, constitute the power of the "master"....

The technical subordination of the workman to the uniform motion of the instruments of labor, and the peculiar composition of the body of workpeople, consisting as it does of individuals of both sexes and of all ages, give rise to a barrack discipline, which is elaborated into a complete system in the factory, and which fully develops the beforementioned labor of overlooking, thereby dividing the work-people into operatives and overlookers, into private soldiers and sergeants of an industrial army.[42]

Thus labor in its historical development becomes the negation of its own principle, that of creative activity through which man makes himself: instead, man makes himself into an accessory of the machine, a partial function in the mechanism of the instruments of labor which dominate him. But Marx the dialectician sees not only the negation but also, at the same time, the counter-tendency growing with it and because of it.

Modern Industry never looks upon and treats the existing form of a process as final. The technical basis of that industry is therefore revolutionary, while all earlier modes of production were essentially conservative. By means of machinery, chemical processes and other methods, it is continually causing changes not only in the technical basis of production, but also in the functions of the laborers, and in the social combinations of the labor-process. At the same time, it thereby also revolutionizes the division of labor within the society, and incessantly launches masses of capital and of workpeople from one branch of production to another. But if Modern Industry, by its very nature, therefore necessitates variation of labor, fluency of function, universal mobility of the laborer, on the other hand, in its capitalistic form, it reproduces the old division of labor with its ossified particularizations.... This is the negative side. But if, on the one hand, variation of work at present imposes itself after the manner of an overpowering natural law, and with the blindly destructive action of a natural law that meets with resistance at all points, Modern Industry, on the other hand, through its catastrophes imposes the necessity of recognizing, as a fundamental law of production, variation of work, consequently fitness of the laborer for varied work, consequently the greatest possible development of his varied aptitudes. It becomes a question of life and death for society to adapt the mode of production to the normal functioning of this law. Modern Industry, indeed, compels society, under penalty of death, to replace the detail-worker of today, crippled by lifelong repetition of one and the same trivial operation, by the fully developed individual, fit for a variety of labors, ready to face any change of production, and to whom the different social functions he performs, are but so many modes of giving free scope to his own natural and acquiring powers.[43]

Marx explained the pre-conditions which were inevitably bound to lead to the division of labor; and, equally inevitably, the division of labor was bound to lead to the division of common property and the transition to *private ownership*.

> The division of labor implies from the outset the division of *the conditions of labor*, of tools and materials, and thus the splitting-up of accumulated capital among different owners, and thus also the division between capital and labor, and the different forms of property itself. The more the division of labor develops and accumulation grows, the sharper are the forms that this process of differentiation assumes. Labor itself can only exist on the premise of this fragmentation.

> Thus two facts are here revealed. First, the productive forces appear as a world for themselves, quite independent of and divorced from the individuals, alongside the individuals: the reason for this is that the individuals, whose forces they are, exist split up and in opposition to one another, while on the other hand these forces are only real forces in the intercourse and association of these individuals. Thus, on the one hand, we have a totality of productive forces, which have, as it were, taken on a material form and are for the individuals no longer the forces of the individuals but of private property, and hence of the individuals only in so far as they are owners of private property themselves.... On the other hand, standing over against these productive forces, we have the majority of the individuals from whom these forces have been wrested away, and who, robbed thus of all real life-content, have become abstract individuals, but who are, however, only by this fact put into a position to enter into relation with one another as individuals.

> The only connection which still links them with the productive forces and with their own existence—labor—has lost all semblance of self-activity and only sustains their life by stunting it. While in the earlier periods self-activity and the production of material life were separated, in that they devolved on different persons, and while, on account of the narrowness of the individuals themselves, the production of material life was considered as a subordinate mode of self-activity, they now diverge to such an extent that finally material life appears as the end, and what produces this material life, labor (which is not the only possible but, as we see, negative form of self-activity), as the means.[44]

This is a thought that recurs again and again in Marx: material life is the *basis*, but not the *purpose*, of human existence. The fact that labor appears only as a means of sustaining life, no longer as creative activity by which man makes and molds himself, is for Marx a contradiction of the nature of man: when he says, therefore, that economic conditions are more powerful than the individual, that is not, for him, an eternal law but a stage of historical development, the transcending of which is the great task of humanity. The economy must not dominate man: it must be brought under the control of a humanity made up of associated individuals.

The division of labor offers the example

of how, as long as man remains in natural society, that is as long as a cleavage exists between the particular and the common interest, as long therefore as activity is not voluntarily, but naturally, divided, man's own deed becomes an alien power opposed to him, which enslaves him instead of being controlled by him.... This crystallization of social activity, this consolidation of what we ourselves produce into an objective power above us, growing out of our control, thwarting our expectations, bringing to naught our calculations, is one of the chief factors in historical development up till now. And out of this very contradiction between the interest of the individual and that of the community the latter takes an independent form as the *State*, divorced from the real interest of individual and community....

The social power, i.e. the multiplied productive force, which arises through the cooperation of different individuals as it is determined within the division of labor, appears to these individuals, since their cooperation is not voluntary but natural, not as their own united power but as an alien force existing outside them, of the origin and end of which they are ignorant, which they thus cannot control, which on the contrary passes through a peculiar series of phases and stages independent of the will and the action of man, nay even being the prime governor of these. This "estrangement" (to use a term which will be comprehensible to the philosophers) can, of course, only be abolished given two *practical* premises....

Marx thought that these two practical premises were, first, that the contradiction between the great mass of non-property-owning humanity and the existing world of wealth and culture had to become "intolerable," and, secondly, that productive forces had to develop universally and not only in a few countries, "for the reason that without this, only *want* is made general, and with want the struggle for necessities would necessarily be reproduced."[45]

Thus it is the division of labor with all its consequences—private ownership of the means of production and the products of labor, domination of the product over the producer, the totality of productive forces and institutions, State, church, justice, etc., confronting the individual as alien forces, which produce the state Marx called *alienation*. Men, with the exception of a tiny minority engaged in creative activity, cannot recognize themselves in their own works; social production exists as a "fatality exterior to themselves,"[46] creation overshadows the creator, and this "second" nature which man has wrested from original, elementary nature appears even more powerful, even less controllable than the first with its famines, earthquakes, and eruptions. The material relationship has grown beyond all individual things and has become an autonomous power.

In a world of advanced division of labor, of private ownership of the materials, instruments, and products of labor, of institutions and ideologies, of *having* and *ruling*, alienation is generalized: not only the worker who sells his labor but also the employer who appropriates the product of another man's work and the merchant who takes the commodity to market, the "haves" and the "have-nots," the rulers and the ruled, are, in such a world, alienated from their work, from others and from themselves. In many ways it is a world upside down, where objects, appropriated by man, acquire the crazy power of owning men.

> Already in feudal land-ownership the ownership of the earth appears as an alien power ruling over men. The serf is the product of the land. In the same way the heir, the first-born son, belongs to the land. It inherits him.[47]

The worker's alienation is the most extreme form because it is the very nature of his activity for the non-worker, the master, the owner, the idler, alienation is not an activity but a condition.

> It should be noted first that everything which appears to the worker as an *activity of alienation*, appears to the non-worker as a *condition of alienation*.[48]

When, at an earlier stage in history, two tribes met at a pre-arranged place and exchanged gifts, that was not an act of alienation but of encounter, of human approach. As soon as the object that had once been a gift became a commodity, trust gave way to mistrust and generous exchange to calculation. What now passed from hand to hand was no longer the *expression* of a group of people but its *alienation* in the work product, and one side no longer admired the objective and special quality in the object offered by the other but was interested only in its general quality, its *exchange value* weighed against the exchange value of something else.

Originally, exchange "both of human activity within production itself and of *human products* against one another [...] = *species activity* and *species spirit*, whose real, conscious and true existence is *social* activity and *social* enjoyment."[49] When this original exchange becomes commodity exchange, and when common property becomes private property, the real community of men is transformed into a caricature of itself. Commodity exchange mediates social intercourse; the *bond of essential nature* that links one man to another 'appears as an inessential bond'; "instead, man's separation from other men appears as his true existence"; "his power over the object appears as the power of the object over him, the lord of creation appears as the slave of his creation."[50]

The political economy of bourgeois society

> comprehends the community of men, or their active *human* nature, their completion of one another making up their species life, their truly human life, under the form of exchange and commerce...'Society,' says Adam Smith, "is a trading society. Each of its members is a merchant."[51]

In commodity exchange, in trade, objects gain power over men; the object offered to another no longer represents the community that offers it; the trader represents the object he is offering for sale. The face of man disappears behind the merchant's social character mask. The community of *competition*, the trading society, manifests itself as estrangement—as *alienation*.

Just as for the man who takes his commodities to market, the commodity becomes the *subject* and he himself only *a function*, individuals become functionaries—officials—in the hierarchy of social institutions. Other men do not see them as fellow-men having equal rights, but as superiors or subordinates, as holders of a rank, as a small or large unit of power. Every functionary is alienated from every other functionary and all of them are alienated from the simple citizen. Likewise the owner and the man who sells his labor are alienated from one another: and, while in small-scale agriculture and in artisan trade such alienation still retains certain features (which may often be hypocritical) of familiarity and trust, in large-scale industry it is undisguised. In other words, while alienation is the universal characteristic of production based on exchange values and the increasing division of labor which such production entails it assumes its most extreme form in the case of the wage laborer, the man who sells his labor as a commodity—in his relationship to his work product, the work process, and himself.

> In labor for gain the following are inherent: (1) the alienation of work from the working subject, and its arbitrary nature; (2) the arbitrary nature and alienation of the work from its object; (3) the determining of the worker by social wants which, however, are alien to him and a constraint upon him, to which he submits only out of selfish want, out of need, and which for him mean only a source of satisfaction of his needs, just as he exists for society only as a slave of *its* needs; (4) the fact that to the worker the maintenance of his individual existence appears as the purpose of his activity, and his real activity only as a means; that he activates his life in order to gain the means of maintaining his life (means of subsistence).

> Hence, the greater and more formed the power of society appears within the private property relation, the more selfish, unsocial, alienated from his own nature does man become.[52]

In an age when this alienation of man from his nature, this antisocial egoism, this reduction of labor to empty wage-earning, to a "job," has come to be accepted without question, it is doubly important to remind ourselves of Marx's protest against alienation, selfishness, and the deformation of labor, against brutal materialism raised to the status of a principle.

Although workers in the most advanced industrial societies are no longer the wretched slaves they were in Marx's time, we can still recognize the essential truth of hard, concrete formulations such as this:

> We have now considered the act of alienation of practical human activity, labor, from two aspects: (1) the relationship of the worker to the *product of labor* as an alien object which dominates him. This relationship is at the same time the relationship to the sensuous external world, to natural objects as an alien and hostile world; (2) the relationship of the worker to the *act of production* within *labor*. This is the relationship of the worker to his own activity as something alien and not belonging to him, activity as suffering (passivity), strength as powerlessness, creation as emasculation, the *personal* physical and mental energy of the worker, his personal life (for what is life but activity?), as an activity which is directed against himself, independent of him and not belonging to him. This is *self-alienation* as against the above-mentioned alienation of the thing.[53]

Because Marx saw the "species-nature of man" in creative activity, in man's conscious transformation of the outside world and consequently in his all-round *self-realization*, the loss of the creative quality of labor meant to him man's alienation from his species-nature and therefore from himself.

If man's relationship to himself is simply a relationship to a living creature that is obliged to work in order to maintain itself—if his activity is not the universal free play of forces but simply *earning*—if his labor has become a commodity and he merely a thing unto himself, then he ceases, as an individual, to represent mankind.

> ... A direct consequence of the alienation of man from the product of his labor, from his life activity and from his species-life, is that *man is alienated* from other *men*. When man confronts himself he also confronts other *men*. What is true of man's relationship to his work, to the product of his work, and to himself, is also true of his relationship to other men, to their labor, and to the objects of their labor.
>
> In general, the statement that man is alienated from his species-life means that each man is alienated from others, and that each of the others is likewise alienated from human life.
>
> Human alienation, and above all the relation of man to himself, is first realized and expressed in the relationship between each man and other men. Thus in the relationship of alienated labor every man regards other men according to the standards and relationships in which he finds himself placed as a worker.[54]

In a *society of alienation* the relationship of a man with other men is not that of a human being to his fellow human beings but that of a servant to his master, of an exploited man to his exploiter, of a subordinate to his commander, a petitioner to a man of privilege, and so forth, to include all the many ranks and degrees of social status allotted to everyone.

The division of labor within the work process reduces the worker to a component of a massive piece of machinery, to some detailed function which renders the work contentless and its performer a fragment of a man: what he produces does not matter to him, the product of his work is not objectification of his own self but something removed from his grasp.

The social division of labor, which makes one man the owner of materials, instruments of labor, and products, and another man a dispossessed creature who takes his labor to market and merely performs the act of production without having any share in determining it, precludes any *productive community* in which every talent would have an equal chance and where production would be determined, not by profit, but by the common material and intellectual interest in the all-round development of man.

The contradiction between the actual socialization of production and the fragmentation of property among a multitude of private interests denies the producers any control over the movement of their products, subjects them to the autonomous power of the products, and distorts human society into a society ruled by things, where man's works oppose him as something alien to him, an alien world of historical "natural laws," mysterious forces of destiny, powerful institutions, gigantic fetishes.

Marx believed that this "confusion and transposition" of man's nature is historically conditioned and can for that reason be overcome. Certainly the objective conditions of labor, the technical and administrative machinery, take on "an ever more colossal independence" *vis-à-vis* living labor itself, and social wealth opposes labor "in increasingly tremendous proportion as an alien and dominant force." But this "process of transposition" is

> merely *historical* necessity, merely a necessity for the development of the productive forces from a certain historical starting point or basis, but by no means an *absolute* necessity of production; rather, a disappearing one, and the [immanent] result and goal of this process is to abolish this basis itself, as well as this form of the process.[55]

The problem of alienation was for Marx a central problem and not, as is frequently asserted nowadays, a romantic humanist notion of the young Marx, "Marx in his anti-Marxist and pre-Marxist phase." Certainly there was a young Marx and an older one, but there was no such thing as an "anti-Marxist" and a "Marxist" Marx. The *Grundrisse* was written in 1857-1858, when Marx was forty years old: the concept of alienation is as alive in this work as in any previous one. But it is true that the hope that the "objective moments of production can be divested of alienation" is supplanted in the last volume of *Capital*—Marx's last work—by the thought that man can only become a *whole man*, that is to say, a man no longer alienated from himself and his fellow men, when he has advanced beyond the sphere of production for the sake of necessity.

4

THE FETISH CHARACTER OF THE COMMODITY

In the description that follows, Fischer gets to the heart of the circumstance in which capitalist society, centered around commodity production, gives seemingly magical personalities to the products that are manufactured, sold, and bought in our daily lives. This fetish, which is directly expressed in every brand name and advertizing slogan, transforms social relations between people into relations between things. With labor power itself put up for sale, the processes of human labor that produced commodities are ripped from our conscious minds, leaving only the categories of the market to define the value of these goods—and of the qualities of our lives. The resulting social alienation is a form of universal "forgetting" that later Marxist philosophers (most notably Georg Lukács) were to call *reification.—JBF*

The declaration of "inalienable" human rights presupposes a world in which everything has been alienated: let human rights, at least, be kept outside the dirty game. Everything has become a commodity: side by side with the meat market there is the art market, side by side with the car market is the book market, the labor market, the sex market, markets for information, secret services and, of course, public opinion. Above all it is man who becomes a commodity:

Production does not only produce man as a *commodity*, the *human commodity*, man in the form of a *commodity*; in conformity with this situation it produces him as a *mentally* and *physically* dehumanized being....[56]

The worker becomes an ever cheaper commodity the more goods he creates. The *devaluation* of the human world increases in direct relation with the increase in value of the world of things.[57]

The young Marx was wrong when he assumed that the worker must become "cheaper," i.e. more wretched, with the growth of production. But the dictum that the devaluation of the human world increases with the increase in value of the world of things remains valid. We have become so accustomed to living in a world of commodities, where nature is perhaps only a poster for a holiday resort and man only an advertisement for a new product, we exist in such a turmoil of alienated objects offered cheaply for sale, that we hardly ask ourselves any longer what it is that magically transforms objects of necessity (or fashion) into commodities, and what is the true nature of the witches' sabbath, ablaze with neon moons and synthetic constellations, that has become our day-to-day reality.

What, then, is a commodity?

> A commodity is in the first place an object outside us, a thing that by its properties satisfies human wants of some sort or another. The nature of such wants, whether, for instance, they spring from the stomach or from fancy, makes no difference. Neither are we here concerned to know how the object satisfies these wants, whether directly as means of subsistence or indirectly as means of production....
>
> The utility of a thing makes it a use-value.... This property of a commodity is independent of the amount of labor required to appropriate its useful qualities.... Use-values become a reality only by use or consumption: they also constitute the substance of all wealth, whatever may be the social form of that wealth. In the form of society we are about to consider, they are, in addition, the material depositories of exchange value.[58]

Between the use-values of objects—bread or drugs, dwelling-houses or weapons—nothing is comparable; the only thing they have in common is that they are used for consumption, production, or destruction. But as exchange values—as commodities—objects are reduced to something comparable, measurable, common to them all.

> This common "something" cannot be either a geological, a chemical, or any other natural property of commodities. Such properties claim our attention only in so far as they affect the utility of those commodities, make them use-values. But the exchange of commodities is evidently an act characterized by a total abstraction from use-value....
>
> As use-values, commodities are, above all, of different qualities, but as exchange-values they are merely different quantities, and consequently do not contain an atom of use-value.
>
> If then we leave out of consideration the use-value of commodities, they have only one common property left, that of being products of labor. But even the product of labor has undergone a change in our hands....

When a table, a house, or a bale of cotton are mutually exchanged in a certain, by no means arbitrary, ratio, all their sensuous properties are wiped out by this act (although it has previously been ascertained that they possess these sensuous properties in the desired quantity, i.e. that the apple is not rotten and the table not badly made). In the act of exchange all these useful characteristics of the work product have not disappeared, and neither have the concrete forms of the labor required for their production: rather, they are all reduced to one, and the same sort of labor, human labor in the abstract.

Let us now consider the residue of each of these products: it consists of the same unsubstantial reality in each, a mere congelation of homogeneous human labor, of labor-power expended without regard to the mode of its expenditure. All that these things now tell us is, that human power has been expended in their production, that human labor is embodied in them. When looked at as crystals of this social substance, common to them all, they are—Values.[59]

(It would take up too much space to comment, even tentatively, on Marx's highly complex theory of exchange value, the objections raised to it, and the attempts made to refute it. We are deliberately confining ourselves to the enigmatic fetish character of the commodity as one of the concrete manifestations of the general alienation which is the result and the precondition of a society based on commodity production.)

A commodity appears, at first sight, a very trivial thing, and easily understood. Its analysis shows that it is, in reality, a very queer thing, abounding in metaphysical subtleties and theological niceties.... So far as it is a value in use, there is nothing mysterious about it.... The form of wood, for instance, is altered by making a table out of it. Yet, for all that, the table continues to be that common, everyday thing, wood. But, so soon as it steps forth as a commodity, it is changed into something transcendent. It not only stands with its feet on the ground, but, in relation to all other commodities, it stands on its head, and evolves out of its wooden brain grotesque ideas, far more wonderful than "table-turning" ever was.[60]

A motor-car as use-value has nothing enigmatic about it but as a commodity it is so capricious and unaccountable that not only the buyer but also, and especially, the producer is confronted with new riddles at every step. Only yesterday the demand was all for great big pompous limousines as status symbols: today, all of a sudden, they have become unsaleable; the plain-looking, solid family car is all the rage; then suddenly this too begins to falter, and firms which dominated the market are faced with collapse. Market analysis, psychology, and publicity keep the commodity under some sort of control: then, quite unexpectedly, it begins to behave in a way "far more wonderful than table-turning ever was."

This willfulness of the commodity is an expression of the contradiction between the *social* nature of production and the apparently "independent" producer. This so-called independent producer is, whether he wants it or not, dependent on the social totality, on the price of raw materials and labor, on the average productivity of labor, on demand and supply, on the consumers' requirements and purchasing power. Thus the commodity becomes the objectification of the inner contradiction of "private economy" in a world of all-embracing social production.

> There is a definite social relation between men, that assumes, in their eyes, the fantastic form of a relation between things. In order, therefore, to find an analogy, we must have recourse to the mist-enveloped regions of the religious world. In that world the productions of the human brain appear as independent beings endowed with life, and entering into relations both with one another and the human race. So it is in the world of commodities with the products of men's hands. This I call the Fetishism which attaches itself to the products of labor, so soon as they are produced as commodities, and which is therefore inseparable from the production of commodities....
> ... articles of utility become commodities, only because they are products of the labor of private individuals or groups of individuals who carry on their work independently of each other. The sum total of the labor of all these private individuals forms the aggregate labor of society. Since the producers do not come into social contact with each other until they exchange their products, the specific social character of each producer's labor does not show itself except in the act of exchange. In other words, the labor of the individual asserts itself as a part of the labor of society, only by means of the relations which the act of exchange establishes directly between the products, and indirectly, through them, between the producers. To the latter, therefore, the relations connecting the labor of one individual with that of the rest appear, not as direct social relations between individuals at work, but as what they really are, material relations between persons and social relations between things.[61]

It is in the commodity that the doubling—or rather, tripling—of the world by human activity manifests itself. A commodity is an object of *nature*, made out of nature's elements. It is a product of *labor*, that is to say, an object designed and formed by man to serve a specific purpose. And it is an object that lets in the "super-sensory," the *social*, the structure of a society based on private property and the division of labor. In this threefold reality it hides the secret of a still deeper contradiction: it is the *single* thing that relates— without its owner's knowledge—to a whole, a private thing that socializes itself. Even when it appears most individual, it relates to general demand and general labor. It brings profit today and disaster tomorrow; its price rises and falls, its value is diminished because a more productive method of work has been introduced somewhere else; it is wooed when it has no rivals, rejected when it has too many, it can start a crisis or even a war, and its possessor seems to be obsessed by it.

The more all-embracing the total labor (and total demand) of human beings on the one hand and the more complex and manifold the division of labor on the other, the greater becomes the power of the densely woven, opaque relationships between things. The social character of labor prevails in the commodity form of the work products. Quite often it will defeat the plans of the private producer or owner, make nonsense of his calculations, sweep everything before it like a force of nature, correct by catastrophe the false relationship between the totality of labor and demand, on the one hand, and the arbitrariness of *having* on the other. The work product as commodity has overpowered its producer, and, by objectifying all relationships, has dehumanized them.

In simpler social structures, in the past, the relationships between people had not been rendered invisible by the relationships between things. In medieval Europe the dependence of the serf on the lord of the manor, of the vassal on the feudal lord, had not yet been transformed into apparent independence hemmed in on all sides by material relations.

> Personal dependence here characterizes the social relations of production just as much as it does the other spheres of life organized on the basis of that production. But for the very reason that personal dependence forms the ground-work of society, there is no necessity for labor and its products to assume a fantastic form different from their reality. They take the shape, in the transactions of society, of services in kind and payments in kind. Here the particular and natural form of labor, and not, as in society based on production of commodities, its general abstract form is the immediate social form of labor. Compulsory labor is just as properly measured by time, as commodity-producing labor; but every serf knows that what he expends in the service of the lord is a definite quantity of his own personal labor-power. The tithe to be rendered to the priest is more matter of fact than his blessing. No matter, then, what we may think of the parts played by the different classes of people themselves in

this society; the social relations between individuals in the performance of their labor, appear at all events as their own mutual personal relations, and are not disguised under the shape of social relations between the products of labor.[62]

Marx certainly felt no nostalgia for this state of affairs; he saw the *materialization of power*, despite all its negative features, as that social form, "wherein a system of universal social metabolism, of universal relationships, many-sided needs, and universal capacities first comes into being,"[63] as the historical transition to a society of free individuals on the basis of their communal, social productivity. But he was anxious to render visible the human beings at work behind the material relations.

> Commodities cannot go to market and make exchanges of their own account. We must, therefore, have recourse to their guardians, who are also their owners.... In order that these objects may enter into relation with each other as commodities, their guardians must place themselves in relation to one another, as persons whose will resides in those objects, and must behave in such a way that each does not appropriate the commodity of the other, and part with his own, except by means of an act done by mutual consent.... The persons exist for one another merely as representatives of, and, therefore, as owners of commodities. In the course of our investigation we shall find, in general, that the characters who appear on the economic stage are but the personifications of the economic relations that exist between them.[64]

The important thing is not the individual commodity owner who obeys the law of the commodity because otherwise it would refuse him the right of ownership; important are the economic conditions which, though they are more powerful than any individual, can only be changed, transformed, revolutionized by united individuals.

Today no one thinks it an ultra-radical notion to suggest that the commodity owner in the world of modern productive forces should not simply be the representative, the spokesman of *his* commodity: that it is necessary to introduce at least a minimum of coordination between labor and demand on the one hand and private interest on the other; that the market cannot be the only regulator, that the commodity cannot be allowed to cause havoc in the name of freedom. The idea of planning is taking root.

But the commodity as a form of alienation will only be abolished when wealth and poverty, extravagance and misery, the power of the few to dispose of the production of the many and the subjugation of the many to the silent or grandiloquent rule of the few, have ceased to confront one another and the world has become a totality: when shortage is no longer the dictator: when plenty has been achieved as the fruit of labor liberated and united by science, the communal spirit, and the co-determination of all.

Today we are still ruled by the commodity and its abstraction—money.

The power of things over men in a society based on commodity production is concentrated in the power of money: of gold.

> ... damned earth,
> Thou common whore of mankind, that putt'st odds
> Among the rout of nations ...
>
> O thou sweet king-killer, and dear divorce
> 'Twixt natural son and sire! thou bright defiler
> Of Hymen's purest bed! thou valiant Mars!
> Thou ever young, fresh, lov'd, and delicate wooer,
> Whose blush doth thaw the consecrated snow
> That lies on Dian's lap! thou visible god,
> That solder'st close impossibilities,
> And mak'st them kiss!

It was not a red revolutionary, but William Shakespeare who wrote those lines. Marx quoted them, adding:

> Since money, as the existing and active concept of value, confounds and exchanges everything, it is the universal *confusion and transportation* of all things, the inverted world, the confusion and transposition of all natural and human qualities.[65]

Marx has an answer to this depersonalization, this alienation and dehumanization by money, which is the measure and the commodity of all commodities.

> Let us assume man to be *man*, and his relation to the world to be a human one. Then love can only be exchanged for love, trust for trust, etc. If you wish to enjoy art you must be an artistically cultivated person; if you wish to influence other people you must be a person who really has a stimulating and encouraging effect upon others. Every one of your relations to man and to nature must be a *specific expression*, corresponding to the object of your will, of your *real individual* life. If you love without evoking love in return, i.e. if you are not able, by the *manifestation* of yourself as a loving person, to make yourself a *beloved* person, then your love is impotent and a misfortune.[66]

But where is the force that can "assume man to be man" and transform a world of fetishes, of confusion and transposition of all values, into a human world?

5
CLASSES AND THE CLASS STRUGGLE

The history of all hitherto existing society is the history of class struggle.[67]

One common distortion of Marx's thought contends that he adopted a mechanical and simplistic formula of a two-class society—capitalist class and proletariat—around which he organized his entire social analysis. According to this view, Marx contended that the various middle or intermediate classes (those classes falling between the bourgeoisie and the proletariat) would simply disappear—i.e. would be absorbed by one or the other of the two polar classes.

Fischer exposes the shallowness of this interpretation. "Marx," he tells us, "refused to offer a simple definition or a ready-made formula in answer to the question: What is a class?" As can be seen in his more concrete historical works, such as *The Eighteenth Brumaire of Louis Bonaparte*, Marx took pains to capture the complexities of the societies he analyzed, with middle and intermediate strata of all kinds receiving significant consideration. Nevertheless, Marx was convinced that the struggle over the future of society would come down to a struggle between the class of owners, managers, and their various hangers-on, and the great majority of working people who had little vested interest in the present society.

Marx identified with the proletariat because it was the only class in society that raised the prospect of revolution (that is, of a future society beyond the present one), and because for the first time in human history a forward-looking, revolutionary social class had emerged that was made up of the great majority, thus raising the possibility of the transcendence of class divisions altogether.—*JBF*

Marx was not the discoverer, still less the "inventor" of classes and of the class struggle. That such things exist was already known to Livy, Machiavelli, Adam Smith, Sismondi, Thierry, Guizot, Thiers, Carlyle, and many other historians, economists, and sociologists. Only in the Germany and Austria of the Holy Alliance, that hodge-podge of princely courts and

74

cottages, privileges and backwardness, guilds and censorship, state occasions and states of emergency, were classes unknown or ignored, and the class struggle was seen as the machination of subversive foreigners.*

Marx's contribution to the theory of classes and class struggle consisted in the following:

1. The attempt to determine the characteristics of a class.
2. The analysis of the origin of classes.
3. The recognition that the interests of one class at any given time coincide with the development of the productive forces and their impulse towards new social structures, while other classes defend the established and the traditional because these correspond to their interests.
4. The conviction that the proletariat is the last of the classes and that its liberation demands the abolition of all classes and the classless, rulerless society.

The social division of labor has given rise to the formation of professional groups of all kinds and, after a lengthy development, of *classes*.

Smiths, potters, carpenters, tailors, cobblers, stonemasons, etc.—all of them artisans—were able to constitute themselves as a class under specific historical conditions, those of the medieval town. In modern society they no longer form a class; they are wage laborers, entrepreneurs or "self-employed" workers employing no hired help.

Doctors, teachers, philosophers, writers, artists are all "intellectuals," but the "intelligentsia" is not a class.

Landowners, yeoman farmers, villeins, serfs, agricultural laborers are in a position of antagonism against town dwellers; yet they do not form a class. The class division cuts across them.

> In the earlier epochs of history, we find almost everywhere a complicated arrangement of society into various orders, a manifold gradation of social rank. In ancient Rome we have patricians, knights, plebeians, slaves; in the Middle Ages, feudal lords, vassals, guildmasters, journeymen, apprentices, serfs; in almost all these classes, again, subordinate gradations.

---

* *The Holy Alliance*: an anti-revolutionary front formed by the German, Austrian, and Czarist Russian governments in 1815.

The modern bourgeois society that has sprouted from the ruins of feudal society has not done away with class antagonisms. It has but established new classes, new conditions of oppression, new forms of struggle in place of the old ones.

Our epoch, the epoch of the bourgeoisie, possesses, however, this distinctive feature: it has simplified the class antagonisms. Society as a whole is more and more splitting up into two great hostile camps, into two great classes directly facing each other: Bourgeoisie and Proletariat.[68]

Later, Marx was to correct this oversimplification, taking greater account of the multiplicity of society and defining more clearly the special characteristics of the most important classes.

But in the first place let it be emphasized that classes are not rigid nor unchangeable, nor are they something given from the beginning of time, but products of historical development, while also being the motive forces of that development.

From the "chartered burgesses" of the earliest towns developed "the first elements of the bourgeoisie":

... Out of the many local corporations of burghers there arose only gradually the burgher *class*. The conditions of life of the individual burghers became, on account of their antagonism to the existing relationships and of the mode of labor determined by these, conditions which were common to them all and independent of each individual. The burghers had created the conditions in so far as they had torn themselves free from feudal ties, and were created by them in so far as they were determined by their antagonism to the feudal system which they found in existence. When the individual towns began to enter into associations, these common conditions developed into class conditions. The same conditions, the same antagonisms, the same interests necessarily called forth on the whole similar customs everywhere. The bourgeoisie itself, with its conditions, develops only gradually, splits according to the division of labor into various fractions and finally absorbs all earlier possessing classes (while it develops the majority of the earlier non-possessing, and a part of the earlier possessing, classes into a new class, the proletariat) in the measure to which all earlier property is transformed into industrial or commercial capital. The separate individuals form a class only in so far as they have to carry on a common battle against another class; otherwise they are on hostile terms with each other as competitors. On the other hand, the class in its turn achieves an independent existence over against the individuals, so that the latter find their conditions of existence predestined, and hence have their position in life and their personal development assigned to them by their class, become subsumed under it.[69]

The important points here are that classes develop out of common special interests in order to wage a common battle against other common special interests which are antagonistic to theirs and which have been elevated to the status of "general" interests; that this battle is necessary for the classes to be able to constitute themselves as such; that in the battle, diverse strata of the population are drawn in and absorbed into the class being constituted; that classes formed in this way are in a constant state of inner movement, splitting up into fractions, becoming reunited under new conditions; that class interests assume an independent character *vis-à-vis* separate individuals, and the antagonism is always being in practice destroyed and created; in short, that classes are not immutable, monolithic formations but are forever changing, developing, differentiating themselves, while at the same time the common element always comes to the fore and integrates the individual within the class.

> Each step in the development of the bourgeoisie was accompanied by a corresponding political advance of that class. An oppressed class under the sway of the feudal nobility, an armed and self-governing association in the medieval commune ("Commune" was the name taken, in France, by the nascent towns even before they had conquered from their feudal lords and masters local self-government and political rights as the "Third Estate"); here independent urban republic (as in Italy and Germany), there taxable "third estate" of the monarchy (as in France), afterwards, in the period of manufacture proper, serving either the semifeudal or the absolute monarchy as a counterpose against the nobility, and, in fact, cornerstone of the great monarchies in general, the bourgeoisie has at last, since the establishment of Modern Industry and of the world market, conquered for itself, in the modern representative State, exclusive political sway.[70]

Not only the bourgeoisie but the proletariat, too, has gone through a lengthy history of development, a history which is as yet by no means concluded. "The bourgeoisie begins with a proletariat which is itself a relic of the proletariat of feudal times."[71]

Runaway serfs, dispossessed peasants, poverty-stricken artisans and journeymen, beggars, tramps, "outsiders" first deprived of work and then herded together in workhouses—it was the poor, to put it quite simply, who formed the original proletariat.

> In the last third of the fifteenth, and the first decade of the sixteenth century ... a mass of free proletarians was hurled on the labor-market

by the breaking up of the bands of feudal retainers, who, as Sir James Steuart well says, "everywhere uselessly filled house and castle".... The rapid rise of the Flemish wool manufacturers, and the corresponding rise in the price of wool in England, gave the direct impulse to these evictions. The old nobility had been devoured by the great feudal wars. The new nobility was the child of its time, for which money was the power of all powers. Transformation of arable land into sheepwalks was, therefore, its cry.... The dwellings of the peasants and the cottages of the laborers were razed to the ground or doomed to decay....

The process of forcible expropriation of the people received in the sixteenth century a new and frightful impulse from the Reformation, and from the consequent colossal spoliation of the church property. The Catholic church was, at the time of the Reformation, feudal proprietor of a great part of the English land. The suppression of the monasteries, etc., hurled their inmates into the proletariat....

Even in the last decade of the seventeenth century the yeomanry, the class of independent peasants, were more numerous than the class of farmers. They had formed the backbone of Cromwell's strength.... About 1750 the yeomanry had disappeared, and so had, in the last decade of the eighteenth century, the last trace of the common land of the agricultural laborer....

The "glorious Revolution" brought into power, along with William of Orange, the landlord and capitalist appropriators of surplus-value. They inaugurated the new era by practicing on a colossal scale thefts of state lands, thefts that had been hitherto managed more modestly....

The last process of wholesale expropriation of the agricultural population from the soil is, finally, the so-called clearing of estates, i.e. the sweeping men off them. All the English methods hitherto considered culminated in "clearing." As we saw in the picture of modern conditions given in a former chapter, where there are no more independent peasants to get rid of, the "clearing" of cottages begins; so that the agricultural laborers do not find on the soil cultivated by them even the spot necessary for their own housing....

The proletariat created by the breaking up of the bands of feudal retainers and by the forcible expropriation of the people from the soil, this "free" proletariat could not possibly be absorbed by the nascent manufacturers as fast as it was thrown upon the world. On the other hand, these men, suddenly dragged from their wonted mode of life, could not as suddenly adapt themselves to the discipline of their new condition. They were turned *en masse* into beggars, robbers, vagabonds, partly from inclination, in most cases from stress of circumstances. Hence at the end of the fifteenth and during the whole of the sixteenth century, throughout Western Europe a bloody legislation against vagabondage. The fathers of the present working class were chastised for their enforced transformation into vagabonds and paupers....

Thus were the agricultural people, first forcibly expropriated from the soil, driven from their homes, turned into vagabonds, and then whipped, branded, tortured by laws grotesquely terrible, into the discipline necessary for the wage system.

It is not enough that the conditions of labor are concentrated in a mass, in the shape of capital, at the one pole of society, while at the other are grouped masses of men, who have nothing to sell but their labor-power. Neither is it enough that they are compelled to sell it voluntarily. The advance of capitalist production develops a working class, which by education, tradition, habit, looks upon the conditions of that mode of production as self-evident laws of Nature....

The class of wage-laborers, which arose in the latter half of the fourteenth century, formed then and in the following century only a very small part of the population, well protected in its position by the independent peasant proprietary in the country and the guild-organization in the town....

The private property of the laborer in his means of production is the foundation of petty industry, whether agricultural, manufacturing, or both; petty industry, again, is an essential condition for the development of social production and of the free individuality of the laborer himself....

This mode of production presupposes parcelling of the soil, and scattering of the other means of production.... It is compatible only with a system of production, and a society, moving within narrow and more or less primitive bounds.... At a certain stage of development it brings forth the material agencies for its own dissolution. From that moment new forces and new passions spring up in the bosom of society; but the old social organization fetters them and keeps them down. It must be annihilated; it is annihilated. Its annihilation, the transformation of the individualized and scattered means of production into socially concentrated ones, of the pygmy property of the many into the huge property of the few, the expropriation of the great mass of the people from the soil, from the means of subsistence, and from the means of labor, this fearful and painful expropriation of the people forms the prelude to the history of capitalism.[72]

The proletariat goes through various stages of development. With its birth begins its struggle with the bourgeoisie. At first the contest is carried on by individual laborers, then by the workpeople of a factory, then by the operatives of one trade, in one locality, against the individual bourgeois who directly exploits them. They direct their attacks not against the bourgeois conditions of production, but against the instruments of production themselves; they destroy imported wares that compete with their labor, they smash to pieces machinery, they set factories ablaze, they seek to restore by force the vanished status of the workman of the Middle Ages.

At this stage the laborers still form an incoherent mass scattered over the whole country, and broken up by their mutual competition.... But with the development of industry the proletariat not only increases in number; it becomes concentrated in greater masses, its strength grows, and it feels that strength more ... the collisions between individual workmen and individual bourgeois take more and more the character of collisions between two classes....

Now and then the workers are victorious. but only for a time. The real fruit of their battles lies, not in the immediate result, but in the ever-expanding union of the workers.... It was just this contact that was needed to centralize the numerous local struggles, all of the same character, into one national struggle between classes. But every class struggle is a political struggle....

This organization of the proletarians into a class, and consequently into a political party, is continually being upset again by the competition between the workers themselves. But it ever rises up again, stronger, firmer, mightier. It compels legislative recognition of particular interests of the workers, by taking advantage of the divisions among the bourgeoisie itself....

The advance of industry, whose involuntary promoter is the bourgeoisie, replaces the isolation of the laborers, due to competition, by their revolutionary combination, due to association. The development of Modern Industry, therefore, cuts from under its feet the very foundation on which the bourgeoisie produces and appropriates products. What the bourgeoisie, therefore, produces, above all, is its own grave-diggers.[73]

This view of Marx's of the development of modern classes, given here in an extremely compressed form, outlines the essential features of a class. But much of this view, even if we make allowances for the agitational nature of the Communist Manifesto, is not clearly defined.

The fifty-second chapter of Volume III of *Capital*, Marx's major work, was to be devoted to this problem. Only the beginning of the chapter was written; Marx died before he could complete it. The chapter is entitled "Classes."

The owners merely of labor-power, owners of capital, and land-owners, whose respective sources of income are wages, profit and ground-rent, in other words wage-laborers, capitalists and land-owners, constitute the three big classes of modern society based upon the capitalist mode of production.

In England modern society is indisputably most highly and classically developed in economic structure. Nevertheless, even here the stratification of classes does not appear in its pure form. Middle and intermediate strata even here obliterate lines of demarcation everywhere (although incomparably less in rural districts than in the cities). However, this is immaterial for our analysis....

The first question to be answered is this: What constitutes a class?—and the reply to this follows naturally from the reply to another question, namely: what makes wage-laborers, capitalists, and landlords constitute the three great social classes?

At first glance—the identity of revenues and sources of revenue. There are three great social groups whose members, the individuals forming them, live on wages, profit and ground-rent respectively, on the realization of their labor-power, their capital, and their landed property.

However, from this standpoint, physicians and officials, e.g., would also constitute two classes, for they belong to two distinct social groups, the members of each of these groups receiving their revenue from one and the same source. The same would also be true of the infinite fragmentation of interest and rank into which the division of social labor splits laborers as well as capitalists and landlords—the latter, e.g., into owners of vineyards, farm owners, owners of forests, mine owners and owners of fisheries.

(Here the manuscript breaks off.)[74]

This unfinished chapter is not the only place where Marx draws attention to the multiple aspects of the division of labor and the multitude of "middle and intermediate strata" which everywhere "obliterate the lines of demarcation."

Marx was not a lover of rigid formulas. He was an observer who never overlooked the individual and the specific in his search for general trends of social development. He did not view the crystallization of classes, highly resistant and effective social formations that they are, as a process tending towards a standstill. He always endeavored to grasp it by taking into account the totality of its definitions.

In *The Eighteenth Brumaire of Louis Bonaparte*, one of his most brilliant works, he discusses such processes of change of the "middle and intermediate strata." As against the coalition of the bourgeoisie which had come into being shortly after the revolutionary events of 1848,

a coalition between petty bourgeois and workers had been formed, the so-called *social-democratic* party. The petty bourgeois saw that they were badly rewarded after the June days of 1848, that their material interests were imperilled, and that the democratic guarantees which were to ensure the effectuation of these interests were called in question by the counter-revolution. Accordingly, they came closer to the workers.... From the social demands of the proletariat the revolutionary point was broken off and a democratic turn given to them; from the democratic claims of the petty bourgeoisie the purely political form was stripped off and their social point thrust forward.... The peculiar character of the Social-Democracy is epitomized in the fact that democratic-republican institutions are demanded as a means, not of doing away with two extremes, capital and wage labor, but of weakening their antagonism and transforming it into harmony.

The content of all the proposed measures "is the transformation of society in a democratic way, but a transformation within the bounds of the petty bourgeoisie."[75]

"The bourgeoisie now felt the necessity of making an end of the democratic petty bourgeois, just as a year before it had realized the necessity of settling with the revolutionary proletariat." The "party of Order" consciously conducts the class struggle.

But the democrat, because he represents the petty bourgeoisie, that is, a *transition class*, in which the interests of two classes are simultaneously mutually blunted, imagines himself elevated above class antagonism generally. The democrats concede that a privileged class confronts them, but they, along with all the rest of the nation, form the *people*.[76]

And if the bourgeoisie, which is consciously fighting for its class interests, is victorious, then that means that "the people" have "failed"—any excuse or other—but it is never the admitted fault of the "transition class" which wants to reconcile the irreconcilable, which has one foot on one side of the fence and one on the other, a class which is contradiction incarnate—in short, a class which has ceased to be one.

The phenomenon is even clearer in the case of the French small-holding peasants who supported Napoleon III as they had supported Napoleon I.

After the first revolution had transformed the peasants from semi-villeins [a status just above serfdom] into freeholders, Napoleon confirmed and regulated the conditions on which they could exploit undisturbed the soil of France which had only just fallen to their lot and slake their youthful passion for property.... The economic development of small-holding property has radically changed the relation of the peasants to the other classes of society. Under Napoleon the fragmentation of the land in the countryside supplemented free competition and the beginning of big industry in the towns. The peasant class was the ubiquitous protest against the landed aristocracy which had just been overthrown.... But in the course of the nineteenth century the feudal lords were replaced by urban usurers;

the feudal obligation that went with the land was replaced by the mortgage; aristocratic landed property was replaced by bourgeois capital.... The interests of the peasants, therefore, are no longer, as under Napoleon, in accord with, but in opposition to the interests of the bourgeois order.[77]

The small-holding peasants form a vast mass, the members of which live in similar conditions but without entering into manifold relations with one another.... In so far as millions of families live under economic conditions of existence that separate their mode of life, their interests and their culture from those of the other classes, and put them in hostile opposition to the latter, they form a class. In so far as there is merely a local interconnection among these small-holding peasants, and the identity of their interests begets no community, no national bond and no political organization among them, they do not form a class. They are consequently incapable of enforcing their class interest in their own name, whether through a parliament or through a convention. They cannot represent themselves, they must be represented. Their representative must at the same time appear as their master, as an authority over them, as an unlimited governmental power that protects them against the other classes and sends them rain and sunshine from above.[78]

Detailed analyses of this kind show why Marx refused to offer a simple definition or a ready-made formula in answer to the question: What is a class? They also show why he spoke of the "great," the decisive, the historically determining classes of modern society.

Identity of revenues or of economic living conditions is not sufficient to constitute a social group as a class in the full sense of the word. A passive identity such as this, a community of interest dictated by destiny only, may be defined as a "class in itself" (to use Hegelian terminology); it becomes a "class for itself" only through a series of further determining circumstances, among which Marx counts the transcending of local limitations such as the individual factory, the individual community, the individual country—in other words, association and universality, the coordination and organization made possible thereby, the conscious opposition of the interests of one's own class to that of other classes, resistance, action, and the class struggle. *A class is born in the class struggle.* Only through such struggle does it develop into a social and historical force.

The position within the realm of socially necessary material production is of decisive importance, for without this realm society cannot exist. An army or a bureaucracy can enforce temporary decisions; but the structure of society and its relative stability are determined by groups directly concerned with the means of production, either as owners or as operators. In the process of technological development, small-scale private property of land, tools and materials is increasingly swallowed up by large-scale private property, so that classes of men such as artisans, small-holding peasants, the petty bourgeoisie are quite unable to hold their own as major classes conscious of a common purpose and engaged in a common fight; they refuse to recognize the polarization of society, feel themselves threatened both by capital and by the proletariat, are pulled this way and that on account of their contradictory economic interests, and tend, when the situation becomes critical, to call for a Napoleon, a strong man above the classes.

And so while Marx says that two great classes are increasingly alone in confronting one another—bourgeoisie and proletariat—he does not, when carrying out a concrete analysis, overlook the multitude of "middle and intermediate" classes or the possibility of all kinds of alliances in the class struggle. The important thing is that more and more powerful means of production and more and more colossal capitals are concentrated in fewer and fewer hands, while on the other side the mass of those who own no means of production whatever and are forced to live by selling their labor power is growing incessantly: so that, overshadowing all else, *capital and labor* loom in opposition to one another.

From time to time, under special conditions, middle strata and intermediate classes are able to seize power—but never to retain it. The Jacobins, the party of the radical petty bourgeoisie, were replaced by the Directorate, the Directorate by Napoleon; and once more it was a Napoleon who, in the years after 1848, as the recognized guardian of the bourgeoisie, not only personified but also guaranteed the latter's dominance. Only the owners of massive means of production (land-owners, commercial magnates, industrialists and finance capitalists) can become a *ruling* class. However much the forms of their rule may differ from one another—ranging from the despotic to the democratic—this rule, whatever its form, is always based on their power over the means of production, on the institutions created for the protection of production relations, on the accustomed established order which comes to be thought of simply as "order" (as though without it there would be chaos), on traditions, conventions, laws which confer the status of "holy" and "eternal" upon existing conditions. The ruling class needs an armed executive (and is prepared, in emergencies, to transfer dictatorial powers to that executive), but its principal power is the *objectified power* of the existing property and law relations.

> The ideas of the ruling class are in every epoch the ruling ideas: i.e. the class, which is the ruling material force of society, is at the same time its ruling intellectual force. The class which has the means of material production at its disposal, has control at the same time over the means of mental production, so that thereby, generally speaking, the ideas of those who lack the means of mental production are subject to it.... The individuals composing the ruling class possess among other things consciousness, and therefore think. In so far, therefore, as they rule as a class and determine the extent and compass of an epoch, it is self-evident that they do this in their whole range, hence among other things rule also as thinkers, as producers of ideas, and regulate the production and distribution of the ideas of their age: thus their ideas are the ruling ideas of the epoch.[79]

The division of labor leads to a separation within the ruling class itself, namely as between those who *think* and those who *act.*

> Within this class this cleavage can even develop into a certain opposition and hostility between the two parts, which, however, in the case of a practical collision, in which the class itself is endangered, automatically comes to nothing, in which case there also vanishes the semblance that the ruling ideas were not the ideas of the ruling class and had a power distinct from the power of this class. The existence of revolutionary ideas in a particular period presupposes the existence of a revolutionary class.[80]

Anti-intellectual circles within the labor movement often refer to this passage; but they are apt to overlook that, although "in the case of a practical collision in which the class itself is endangered," the ideas of the ruling class will not contradict that class interest, the "producers of ideas," that is to say the intellectuals, may disavow the ruling class and become its active opponents.

> Finally, in times when the class struggle nears the decisive hour, the process of dissolution going on within the ruling class, in fact within the whole range of old society, assumes such a violent, glaring character, that a small section of the ruling class cuts itself adrift, and joins the revolutionary class, the class that holds the future in its hands. Just as, therefore, at an earlier period, a section of the

nobility went over to the bourgeoisie, so now a portion of the bourgeoisie goes over to the proletariat, and in particular, a portion of the bourgeois ideologists, who have raised themselves to the level of comprehending theoretically the historical movement as a whole.[81]

More than that: those who have come into conflict with the rulers by reason of the very conditions of their existence rarely become a revolutionary class without the help of thinkers who, although they come from quite different spheres of society, "have raised themselves to the level of comprehending theoretically the historical movement as a whole." Marx and Engels were such thinkers.

The ruling class justifies its rule by claiming that it is the representative of law and order, of the moral principle; it claims that it does not rule as a class but as the defender of the "common good":

> The class making a revolution appears from the very start, merely because it is opposed to a *class*, not as a class but as the representative of the whole of society; it appears as the whole mass of society confronting the one ruling class. It can do this because, to start with, its interest really is more connected with the common interest of all other non-ruling classes, because under the pressure of conditions its interest has not yet been able to develop as the particular interest of a particular class. Its victory, therefore, benefits also many individuals of the other classes which are not winning a dominant position, but only in so far as it now puts these individuals in a position to raise themselves into a ruling class. When the French bourgeoisie overthrew the power of the aristocracy it thereby made it possible for many proletarians to raise themselves above the proletariat, but only in so far as they became bourgeois. Every new class, therefore, achieves its hegemony only on a broader basis than that of the class ruling previously, in return for which the opposition of the non-ruling class against the new ruling class later develops all the more sharply and profoundly. Both these things determine the fact that the struggle to be waged against this new ruling class, in its turn, aims at a more decided and radical negation of the previous conditions of society than could all previous classes which sought to rule.[82]

In this simplified exposé the fact that "every new class achieves its hegemony only on a broader basis than that of the class ruling previously" is mentioned only in passing. This "broader basis" is an intrinsic element of progressive social development, and in another context Marx put the strongest emphasis on the historical achievement of the bourgeoisie and its role as constant revolutionizer of the state of the world. In the *Communist Manifesto* we read:

The bourgeoisie cannot exist without constantly revolutionizing the instruments of production, and thereby the relations of production, and with them the whole relations of society. Conservation of the old modes of production in unaltered form, was, on the contrary, the first condition of existence for all earlier industrial classes. Constant revolutionizing of production, uninterrupted disturbance of all social conditions, everlasting uncertainty and agitation distinguish the bourgeois epoch from all earlier ones. All fixed, fast-frozen relations, with their train of ancient and venerable prejudices and opinions, are swept away, all new-formed ones become antiquated before they can ossify. All that is solid melts into air, all that is holy is profaned, and man is at last compelled to face with sober senses, his real conditions of life, and his relations with his kind.[83]

The bourgeoisie has changed since then. At the time when the great capitalist monopolies were created it looked as though the bourgeoisie, turned reactionary, were neither able nor willing to carry on the continual revolutionizing of production, as though mankind were falling victim to an anti-rational ideology which would prevent man from "facing with sober senses his relations with his kind." And yet the continual revolutionizing of production (which attained unexampled scope during the scientific and technical revolution of our century), and the incessant change of all social conditions, has remained characteristic of the bourgeois era. It is precisely the class struggle that keeps the bourgeoisie from becoming set in a rigid pattern.

The working class has changed too. In the advanced capitalist countries it is no longer the wretched proletariat of Marx's time; it has gained in size, differentiation, social status; it is becoming convinced of its ability to be the motive force of production and of social change. Many-layered and contradictory within itself, as a mass of wage and salary earners (workers, employees, technicians, engineers, administrators, scientists) it nevertheless represents an overwhelming majority over the owners of the means of production.

All previous historical movements were movements of minorities, or in the interest of minorities. The proletarian movement is the self-conscious, independent movement of the immense majority, in the interest of the immense majority. The proletariat, the lowest stratum of our present society, cannot stir, cannot raise itself up, without the whole superincumbent strata of official society being sprung into the air.[84]

Turns of phrase like "sprung into the air" should not be taken literally. The basic thought, always recurring in Marx's work, was that the proletariat, which sets all the means of production in motion yet never owns them nor disposes of them, is the *last* class, a class that is constantly growing and is increasingly opposed to the division between labor and capital. In order to liberate itself as a class it must abolish the absurd conditions which make the only productive class of society the ruled class: it must abolish itself as a class, thus abolishing all classes and class rule as such.

In one of the most impressive passages in *Capital,* Marx wrote:

> Along with the constantly diminishing number of the magnates of capital ... grows the mass of misery, oppression, slavery, degradation, exploitation; but with this too grows the revolt of the working class, a class always increasing in numbers, and disciplined, united, organized by the very mechanism of the process of capitalist production itself. The monopoly of production becomes a fetter upon the mode of production, which has sprung up and flourished along with, and under it. Centralization of the means of production and socialization of labor at last reach a point where they become incompatible with their capitalist integument. This integument is burst asunder. The knell of capitalist private property sounds. The expropriators are expropriated.[85]

Later on we shall inquire whether the "mass of misery" has really grown. In the present context, the theory of classes and of the class struggle, which defines the revolutionary class in any given epoch as the pioneer of a new social era (until the creation of a classless and rulerlesss society), leads us directly to the philosophy of history developed by Marx and Engels: the philosophy of historical materialism.

6

HISTORICAL MATERIALISM

In Marx's philosophy of history, each stage of development of the productive forces of society is associated with certain forms of property, with certain relations between human beings and productive conditions. History is conditioned at each stage of its development by the way in which the division of labor and class relations have evolved. Yet, from the mere fact that social relations were conditioned, Marx did not conclude that "destiny is unconditional," as Fischer explains. Historical materialism thus rejects historical fatalism. Marx's method of analysis demanded that social conditions and relations be studied anew in each specific historical setting, since history is not made as an act of human will, "but under circumstances directly encountered, given, and transmitted from the past."—*JBF*

Marx explained in *Capital*:

The capitalist mode of appropriation, the result of the capitalist mode of production, produces capitalist private property. This is the first negation of individual private property, as founded on the labor of the proprietor. But capitalist production begets, with the inexorability of a law of Nature, its own negation. It is the negation of negation. This does not re-establish private property for the producer, but gives him individual property based on the acquisitions of the capitalist era: i.e., on the cooperation and the possession in common of the land and of the means of production.[86]

In his *Preface to A Contribution to the Critique of Political Economy*, Marx wrote—and his formulation has been repeated hundreds of times:

In the social production of their life men enter into definite relations that are indispensable and independent of their will, relations of production which correspond to a definite stage of development of their material productive forces. The sum total of these relations of production constitutes the economic structure of society, the real foundation, on which rises a legal and political superstructure and to which correspond definite forms of social consciousness. The mode

89

of production of material life conditions the social, political and intellectual life process in general. It is not the consciousness of men that determines their being, but, on the contrary, their social being that determines their consciousness. At a certain stage of their development, the material productive forces of society come in conflict with the existing relations of production, or—what is but a legal expression for the same thing—with the property relations within which they have been at work hitherto. From forms of development of the productive forces these relations turn into their fetters. Then begins an epoch of social revolution. With the change of the economic foundation the entire immense superstructure is more or less rapidly transformed. In considering such transformations a distinction should always be made between the material transformation of the economic conditions of production, which can be determined with the precision of natural science, and the legal, political, religious, aesthetic of philosophic—in short, ideological forms in which men become conscious of this conflict and fight it out. Just as our opinion of an individual is not based on what he thinks of himself, so can we not judge of such a period of transformation by its own consciousness; on the contrary, this consciousness must be explained rather from the contradictions of material life, from the existing conflict between the social productive forces and the relations of production.[87]

The philosophy of history proposed here in concentrated form is an entirely new one. It views history neither as an accumulation of accidents, of the deeds of great men, nor as a process of constantly recurring ebbs and tides, an eternally self-repeating pattern—nor as the work of mysterious forces, predestined by some other-worldly plan of redemption or damnation or by the destiny of the World Spirit, but as the development of the human race determined by the nature of *labor*. The division of labor, the growth of productive forces, the association of production and private appropriation give rise, of necessity, to social contradictions. Every given stage of development of the productive forces requires certain specific forms of property, of relations between human beings and relations of production. Without such forms the productive forces cannot function and human society cannot exist. These forms correspond, first of all, to the level of the forces of production; but that level is never at a standstill; the development of the forces of production enters into manifold conflicts with the established relations of production, conflicts which could be resolved by mutual adaptation if antagonistic interests were not involved.

The growth of productive forces is inherent in the nature of labor. The possibility of satisfying not only elementary but even refined needs by the use of new tools, methods and knowledge demands its own realization, especially when the dynamic of capitalist production and competition has been set into motion. (In this connection we should note that Marx draws a clear distinction between *private property* and *individual property*. Individual ownership of objects of necessity or luxury, of clothing, housing, furnishings, of articles of comfort rendered possible by technology, can be secured on the basis of cooperation and common ownership of the land and of the means of production created by labor itself. When Marx speaks of private property he means a form of property which, though social by its very nature, has been deprived of that social character by the affixing of an arbitrary sign which declares it to be *Private*.) Every mode of production carries its own negation within itself. The productive forces themselves burst the integument which is becoming a fetter upon them. A new order, adapted to the new forces of production, comes into being.

This fascinating theory of development of the human race which, though in no way predetermined, nevertheless obeys certain laws, is fraught with the danger of mechanical oversimplification, and it has not escaped that danger. Marx himself, great dialectician though he was, has on occasion provided future Marxists with an excuse for viewing history as an automatically functioning mechanism whose most important components are not living men but dead objects—instruments of labor, machines, object relations. Thus when he wrote, for example, of "the advance of industry, whose involuntary promoter is the bourgeoisie"[88] (*Communist Manifesto*), or said that "capitalist production begets, with the inexorability of a law of Nature, its own negation";[89] when, as he not infrequently did, he described society as "a second Nature" subject to its own immutable natural laws—on these occasions he was unwittingly preparing the ground for oversimplification and misunderstandings.

We read in *The Poverty of Philosophy*:

Social relations are closely bound up with productive forces. In acquiring new productive forces men change their mode of production; and in changing their mode of production, in changing the way of earning their living, they change all their social relations. The hand-mill gives you society with the feudal lord; the steam-mill, society with the industrial capitalist.[90]

Many simplifiers of Marxist theory have deduced from this that the instruments of labor, not the men who use them, are the actual initiators and perpetrators of social change. In this way the productive forces have been *objectified*: once the steam-mill exists, what need is there for the class struggle of the bourgeoisie? And once we have got atomic power stations, surely the new society must come into being of its own accord? It is true that in the same *Poverty of Philosophy* we find a passage which reads:

Of all the instruments of production, the greatest productive power is the revolutionary class itself.[91]

And in *Wage Labor and Capital*, two years later, the same point is made more explicitly: "A Negro is a Negro. He only becomes a slave in certain relations. A cotton-spinning jenny is a machine for spinning cotton. It becomes *capital* only in certain relations. Torn from these relationships it is no more capital than gold in itself is *money* or sugar the price of sugar."[92]

In other words, the instruments of labor, the tools, machines, and so forth, are only a part of the forces of production; men with their technical and social experience, their needs and their insights, the degree of their organization and consciousness, are more important. The steam-mill contributes towards creating a revolutionary class: but it is not the steam-mill that creates the revolutionary ideas which will grip the new class and make of it an active revolutionary class.

... But theory itself becomes a material force when it has seized the masses. Theory is capable of seizing the masses when it demonstrates *ad hominem*, and it demonstrates *ad hominem* as soon as it becomes radical. To be radical is to grasp things by the root. But for man the root is man himself.[93]

Certainly a revolutionary idea or theory can only seize the masses when the material preconditions for this have ripened with society. The root of man is man himself, but man under certain specific social conditions, not divorced from the totality of productive forces and production relations within which he is the conqueror or the victim, the hammer or the anvil.

The works of man have become an alien power apparently independent from man himself, and these object relations follow certain laws which *resemble* the laws of nature; but they differ from them by the fact that the works of man did not make themselves, so that, although they may slip from the hands of their makers, they nevertheless continue to exercise an effect upon him, changing his capacities, his needs, and his whole consciousness, and thus endowing him with the power to appropriate his own creation by transforming it in a revolutionary way.

Marx repeatedly compared the law of motion of history with natural laws, and his critics have repeatedly posed the question: If there is a historical law of development, what is the point of action and the class struggle? If a law of nature takes care of the sequence of social forms, why do we need political parties to organize the battle for socialism? The question is backed by a vulgarization of Marxism which has replaced the comparison between historical and natural laws by an identification of the two. In particular, Karl Kautsky, with his Darwinian background, did much to further the misunderstanding.

As we have already pointed out, there are passages in Marx which make such an interpretation possible. This can no doubt be explained by the influence of Hegel, who said of development that it maintains itself "like an armored phalanx" after the fashion of "the sun in its course"; and Darwin's theory of evolution also had a lasting influence on Marx, who saw in it a direct confirmation of laws of development.

In some passages too much stress is laid on the works of man and too little on man himself and on his interaction with the social world he has created and which has grown beyond his control:

> Although, then, the whole of this movement appears as a social process, and although the separate elements of this movement derive from the conscious will and specific aims of individuals, the totality of the process nevertheless appears as an objective relationship which comes into being naturally: emerging from the clash between conscious individuals, but being neither contained within their consciousness nor subsumed as a whole under them. Their mutual clashes produce a social power which stands above them and is alien to them; their interaction is a process and a force independent of themselves.[94]

However, close study of such passages in conjunction with the overall concept of historical materialism shows that, while Marx occasionally overemphasized the "natural laws" of historical development, he never overlooked the fact that it is men themselves who make their history, even in a world of alienation in which the products of human activity have assumed a ghostly life of their own.

In an article on *The Future Results of British Rule in India*, written on July 22, 1853, this differentiation between the "natural law" which governs society and the activity of revolutionary movements which alter the laws of previous developments is made patently clear.

After describing the "devastating" effects of English industry on India, Marx writes:

> Bourgeois industry and commerce create these material conditions of a new world in the same way as geological revolutions have created the surface of the earth. When a great social revolution shall have mastered the results of the bourgeois epoch, the market of the world and the modern powers of production, and subjected them to the common control of the most advanced peoples, then only will human progress cease to resemble that hideous pagan idol, who would not drink the nectar but from the skulls of the slain.[95]

The passage is of interest not only because it confirms that Marx expected the victory of the socialist revolution to occur more or less simultaneously in the industrially developed countries, and not only because it proves that Marx had left Hegel's idea of a regular and continuous development behind him. It is above all significant in the present context because here the comparison with natural law goes hand in hand with the recognition of a conscious activity of conscious forces.

The same meaning emerges from the "Afterword" to the second edition of *Capital*, where Marx quotes with approval the following text by a Russian commentator:

> As soon as society has outlived a given period of development, and is passing over from one given stage to another, it begins to be subject also to other laws. In a word, economic life offers us a phenomenon analogous to the history of evolution in other branches of biology. The old economists misunderstood the nature of economic laws when they likened them to the laws of physics and chemistry.... With the varying degree of development of productive power, social conditions and the laws governing them vary too.[96]

Marx's concept of history as a whole was based on the conviction that there exists an *objective* development containing within it the formation of a *subjective* factor which is then instrumental in realizing the development. Private property

> drives itself in its economic movement towards its own dissolution, only, however, through a development which does not depend on it, of which it is unconscious and which takes place against its will, through the very nature of things; only inasmuch as it produces the proletariat as proletariat, that misery conscious of its spiritual and physical misery, that dehumanization conscious of its dehumanization and therefore self-abolishing.[97]

The belief in the necessity of development contains within it the belief that an ever-increasing number of human beings will effect the necessary development by free decision. This is not, as Marx's critics often claim, the fundamental contradiction of Marxism: it is the *fundamental idea of Marxist dialectics.*

In our opinion Marx never abandoned the view he proclaimed in *The Holy Family:*

> *History* does *nothing,* it "possesses *no* immense wealth," it "wages *no* battles." It is *man,* real living man, that does all that, that possesses and fights; "history" is not a person apart, using man as means for its own particular aims; history is *nothing but* the activity of man pursuing his aims.[98]

Being not just a socialist thinker, but also a leader of the labor movement, Marx was fully aware of the need to organize those forces whose interest it is to advance a development recognized as necessary:

> The political movement of the working class has as its ultimate object, of course, the conquest of political power for the working class, and for this it is naturally necessary that a previous organization of the working class, arising from its economic struggles, should have been developed up to a certain point....

> Where the working class is not yet far enough advanced in its organization to undertake a decisive campaign against the collective power, that is, the political power, of the ruling classes, it must at any rate be trained for this by continual agitation against the policy of the ruling classes and adopting an attitude hostile to it. Otherwise it will remain a plaything in their hands.... [99]

That is why we find in Marx, side by side with comparisons with natural history whose purpose was doubtless to draw attention to the novelty of his theory, clear indications that he meant social and historical laws to be understood as *laws having the character of tendencies.*

> Under capitalist production, the general law acts as the prevailing tendency only in a very complicated and approximate manner, as a never ascertainable average of ceaseless fluctuations.[100]

A passage from a letter to Dr. Ludwig Kugelmann of April 17, 1871 shows how little inclined Marx was to compare historical development with Hegel's "sun in its course":

> World history would indeed be very easy to make, if the struggle were taken up only on condition of infallibly favorable chances. It would, on the other hand, be of a very mystical nature, if "accidents" played no part. These accidents themselves fall naturally into the general course of development and are compensated again by other accidents. But acceleration and delay are very dependent upon such "accidents," which include the "accident" of the character of those who at first stand at the head of the movement.[101]

Even laws of nature are only an expression of maximum probability. The laws of social movement have the character of tendencies. What happens does not have to have happened.

In *The Eighteenth Brumaire of Louis Bonaparte*, Marx analyzes in great detail the social situation and the economic and class preconditions for an adventurer's rise to dictatorship:

> It is not enough to say, as the French do, that their nation was taken unawares. A nation and a woman are not forgiven the unguarded hour in which the first adventurer that comes along could violate them.... It remains to be explained how a nation of thirty-six millions can be surprised and delivered unresisting into captivity by three high-class swindlers.[102]

The explanation is supplied with a natural scientist's precision. But then Marx goes on to describe Napoleon III's political defeat of March 10, 1850, adding:

> The party of Order proved unable to take advantage of this opportunity that would never return. Instead of boldly possessing itself of the power offered, it did not even compel Bonaparte to reinstate the ministry dismissed on November 1.... The social-democratic party, for its part, seemed only to try to find pretexts for putting its own victory once again in doubt and for blunting its point.... Instead of ... forcing the adversary to fight at the moment of popular enthusiasm and favorable mood in the army, the democratic party wearied Paris during the months of March and April with a new election campaign, let the aroused popular passions wear themselves out in this repeated provisional election game, let the revolutionary energy satiate

itself with constitutional successes, dissipate itself in petty intrigues, hollow decimations and sham movements.[103]

We see that Marx analyzes not only the laws of the development but also those situations in which an alternative offered itself. Similarly we may say that the tendency toward fascism during the years of the great slump was immensely strong, yet Hitler's triumph was by no means due to a social "law of nature." Marx's philosophy of history is not historical fatalism; it does not exclude the alternative; from the fact that *decisions are conditioned*, it does not deduce that *destiny is unconditional*.

Like the problem of the laws of development, the mutual relationship between "base" and "superstructure" has been mechanically misunderstood not only by Marx's critics but also by many of his followers; and the misunderstanding still continues.

Intellectual production does not follow material production but occurs simultaneously and in constant interaction with it. What emerges as the "superstructure" is a totality of prescriptions and prohibitions, laws, institutions, judgements, and prejudices which corresponds to the economic structure of society, the degree of division of labor and the interests of the class which, by reason of the division of labor, has become the ruling class at that time. Hence the ideas of the rulers are the dominant ideas, but not the only ones, of the epoch. Marx stressed again and again that every new society carries its own negation within itself, the inner contradiction which finds its most striking expression in the class struggle. Every new society is therefore the negation of the preceding one, whose habits, ideas and notions continue to exist deep within it. "The tradition of all the dead generations weighs like a nightmare on the brain of the living."[104]

And at the same time the future society ripens as a negation inside the existing one, conditioned by the growth of the material and spiritual forces of production. Thus the dominant ideas are always permeated by other, rebellious ones, which may be forward- or backward-looking, so that the class struggle is fought not only as an economic but also as a political and intellectual battle. Marx and Engels repeatedly denied that economic conditions and demands, although "in the last instance" primary, should be seen as the *only* historical driving forces; they denied that *every* historical movement, *every* political event, *every* philosophic idea must be directly and exclusively ascribed to economic processes.

And so the architectural concept of "base" and "superstructure" should not lead to the notion that society is like a building of which first the economic foundations must be laid (in the hope, perhaps, that the stones will arrange themselves into a "base" of their own accord), to be followed by the superstructure, one floor succeeding the next all the way up to the roof, as if in obedience to the law of gravity and the architect's command. Only a parrot schoolboy utterly devoid of imagination can get by with the ever-available quotation that social being determines consciousness and not the other way about. Whenever he analyzed a concrete political situation Marx made it clear that social being is more than just the sum of economic conditions. Conditions are affected by many elements of consciousness—true, false or clouded consciousness. Since men are beings endowed with consciousness there is no rigid frontier between consciousness and social being. The essential thing about the philosophy of history developed by Marx is that it always proceeds from *social reality*, not from abstract categories: from the "simple material production of life," not from intellectual constructs: from practice, not from a set of self-generating, self-developing, self-resolved ideas.

> Our conception of history depends on our ability to expound the real process of production, starting out from the simple material production of life, and to comprehend the form of intercourse★ connected with this and created by this (i.e. civil society in its various stages), as the basis of all history; further, to show it in its action as State; and so, from this starting-point, to explain the whole mass of different theoretical products and forms of consciousness, religion, philosophy, ethics, etc., etc., and trace their origins and growth, by which means, of course, the whole thing can be shown in its totality (and therefore, too, the reciprocal action of these various sides on one another). It has not, like the idealistic view of history, in every period

---

★ In later works Marx replaced the concept of "intercourse" with that of "production relations."

to look for a category, but remains constantly on the real ground of history.... It shows that history does not end by being resolved into "self-consciousness" as "spirit of the spirit," but that in it at each stage there is found a material result: a sum of productive forces, a historically created relation of individuals to nature and to one another, which is handed down to each generation from its predecessor; a mass of productive forces, different forms of capital, and conditions, which, indeed, is modified by the new generation on the one hand, but also on the other prescribes for it its conditions of life and gives it a definite development, a special character. It shows that circumstances make men just as much as men make circumstances.[105]

In the *Theses on Feuerbach*, Marx's polemic against the shortcomings of previous materialist doctrine which overlooked the active side of man and ignored human *practice* as the world-changing activity, Marx repeats the same thought:

The materialistic doctrine concerning the changing of circumstances and education forgets that circumstances are changed by men and that the educator himself must be educated.... The coincidence of the changing of circumstances and of human activity or self-changing can only be comprehended and rationally understood as *revolutionary practice*.[106]

Revolutionary practice changes circumstances and changes man himself. It sees man not only as the object of history but also as its subject: he is an object capable, by subjective activity, of becoming a subject and of changing existing circumstances. It is in the recognition of this constant interaction between man and his works, between social "laws of nature" and the nature of man as a being capable of changing the circumstances he finds around him, between production relations which tend to conserve what has already been achieved and material and intellectual productive forces which press inexorably forward, that we find the quintessence and the culmination of historical materialism.

Men make their own history, but they do not make it just as they please; they do not make it under circumstances chosen by themselves, but under circumstances directly encountered, given and transmitted from the past.[107]

7
VALUE AND SURPLUS VALUE

For Marx, it was a matter-of-fact reality of capitalist society that labor power (the capacity to work) was treated as a commodity virtually like any other. Like commodities in general, the value of labor power was determined by the cost of reproducing it. In the case of labor power these costs were equal to an historically determined level of subsistence (varying with custom, level of development, the current state of class struggle, etc.). The amount of time per working day spent creating the value necessary to reproduce the wages of the workers was referred to as *necessary labor-time*. The remainder of the working day Marx called *surplus labor-time*. It was the latter that was the source of the surplus value (or gross profits) of the capitalist. Surplus value could thus be viewed as a residual, consisting of the additional value added in production after wage costs were accounted for. The relationship between capitalist and worker is defined as a struggle over how much of the value created by the worker's labor, measured in labor-time—beyond the labor-time it takes to produce the wages necessary for the worker's subsistence—is claimed by the capitalist employer (usually as some kind of formal entity, a firm or corporation) as its own in the form of profit. The ratio defined by the relation of surplus to necessary labor-time was described by Marx as the "rate of exploitation" (or "rate of surplus value").

Although the capitalist is presented in Marx's analysis as someone who is concerned principally with expanding the proportion of surplus labor-time (generating gross profits) and reducing the proportion of necessary labor-time (the work input necessary for generating wage payments), Marx warns against the view that every capitalist is a villain. Rather, he characterizes the capitalist more abstractly as "capital personified," i.e. as a representative of capital as a social relation. In reality individuals may depart from this description, and resist some aspects of their social role. Marx's analysis is less inclined than any other to place the blame on the individual.—*JBF*

Even the most simplified summary of the economic ideas Marx developed in *Capital*—his major work—as well as in *Wages, Price, and Profit*, the *Grundrisse*, *A Contribution to the Critique of Political Economy*, *Theories of Surplus Value*, *Wage*

Labor and Capital, and in many other writings, would require a separate book in itself, not to mention the many and complex objections to these ideas raised by Marx's critics and the replies given, in part, by Marx himself in anticipation of such criticisms. We are obliged in this chapter to confine ourselves to formulating and explaining a few basic concepts, most of which we have already had occasion to touch upon in earlier chapters.

We remind our readers of Chapter 4 ("The Fetish Character of the Commodity") and repeat: Every commodity must first of all satisfy a need; it must be useful; that is to say, it must have a *use-value*.

In a developed system of commodity exchange it is found that useful objects—use-values—are mutually exchangeable, not in an arbitrary manner but in accordance with a *measure* or law common to all objects once they have been transformed into commodities. Although fluctuations are unavoidable because of excessive or insufficient supply, price pushing, speculation, etc., these fluctuations nevertheless occur around a certain magnitude which always asserts itself as the secret of the object-as-commodity.

Marx points out that Aristotle already saw the exchange of commodities in accordance with a certain measure—a simple and natural thing on the face of it—as something highly enigmatic.

"'Exchange,' he says, 'cannot take place without equality, and equality not without commensurability.' Here, however, he comes to a stop, and gives up the further analysis of the form of value. 'It is, however, in reality, impossible that such unlike things can be commensurable'—i.e., qualitatively equal. Such an equalization can only be something foreign to their real nature, consequently only 'a makeshift for practical purposes.'" And Marx provides the answer: the "common substance" Aristotle looked for but failed to find is *human labor*.

> There was, however, an important fact which prevented Aristotle from seeing that, to attribute value to commodities, is merely a mode of expressing all labor as equal human labor, and consequently as labor of equal quality. Greek society was founded upon slavery, and had, therefore, for its natural basis, the inequality of men and of their labor-powers. The secret of the expression of value, namely, that all

kinds of labor are equal and equivalent, and so far as they are human labor in general, cannot be deciphered, until the notion of human equality has already acquired the fixity of a popular prejudice. This, however, is possible only in a society in which the great mass of the produce of labor takes the form of commodities, in which, consequently, the dominant relation between man and man is that of owners of commodities.[108]

When we speak of the value of a commodity, then, we mean its exchange value. The value of a coat is greater than that of the fabric of which it is made, the value of the fabric greater than that of the wool, yarn, natural or artificial fiber of which it consists. This value increase can only be explained by the fact that something has been added at every stage: yet nothing has been added except human labor. It is by the quantity of labor involved that the value of a commodity is measured; and the quantity itself is measured by the time spent on labor.

Some people might think that if the value of a commodity is determined by the quantity of labor spent on it, the more idle and unskillful the laborer, the more valuable would his commodity be, because more time would be required in its production. The labor, however, that forms the substance of value, is homogeneous human labor, expenditure of one uniform labor-power. The total labor-power of society, which is embodied in the sum total of the values of all commodities produced by that society, counts here as one homogeneous mass of human labor-power, composed though it be of innumerable individual units. Each of these units is the same as any other, so far as it has the character of the average labor-power of society, and takes effect as such; that is, so far as it requires for producing a commodity, no more time than is needed on an average, no more than is socially necessary.[109]

"The value of one commodity is to the value of any other, as the labor-time necessary for the production of the one is to that necessary for the production of the other." Having said this, Marx immediately reformulates it in a more striking form: "As values, all commodities are only definite masses of congealed labor-time."[110] The image does not merely suggest how living labor congeals into a dead object: the association with dripping sweat and congealed blood is almost inescapable.

Is, then, every kind of labor equal to every other kind— skilled labor to unskilled, simple labor to that which presupposes specialized knowledge? Marx distinguishes between *simple average labor* which, though it changes its character from one country and one culture to another, is nevertheless a given thing in any existing society, and *skilled labor*.

But

> skilled labor counts only as simple labor intensified, or rather, as multiplied simple labor, a given quantity of skilled being considered equal to a greater quantity of simple labor. Experience shows that this reduction is constantly being made.[111] ... All labor of a higher or more complicated character than average labor is expenditure of labor-power of a more costly kind, labor-power whose production has cost more time and labor, and which therefore has a higher value, than unskilled or simple labor-power.[112]

Developed commodity exchange demands a universal equivalent, a commodity which serves as the standard for all commodities and, as such, acquires "real consistence and general social validity." Gold and silver—money—have been made into this universal equivalent.[113]

> Money is a crystal formed of necessity in the course of the exchanges, whereby different products of labor are practically equated to one another and thus by practice converted into commodities. The historical progress and extension of exchanges develops the contrast, latent in commodities, between use-value and value.[114]

Use-value becomes the determining value only in extreme situations; as a general rule, it is exchange value which—as "congealed labor-time"—makes up the value of a commodity.

The *value* of a commodity is not identical with its *price*; but prices are connected, however elastically, with value, circling it as electrons circle the nucleus of the atom.

Socially necessary labor of equal magnitude can be expressed by different prices. These prices may be

> too small or too great properly to express the magnitude of the wheat's value, nevertheless they are its prices, for they are, in the first place, the form under which its value appears, i.e. money; and in the second place, the exponents of its exchange-ratio with money.... But this exchange-ratio may express either the real magnitude of that commodity's value, or the quantity of gold deviating from that value, for which, according to circumstances, it may be parted with. The possibility, therefore, of quantitative incongruity between price and magnitude of value, or the deviation of the former from the latter, is inherent in the price-form itself. This is no defect, but, on the contrary, admirably adapts the price-form to a mode or production whose inherent laws impose themselves only as the mean of apparently lawless irregularities that compensate one another.[115]

Here a comparison with natural science is not out of place. The rule of molecular movement exists only as a blindly arbitrary average rule of lawlessness. In production, the social character of the production process asserts itself as the value of the commodity determined by the quantity of socially necessary labor-time; the price expresses the accidental nature of the market and the planlessness of an economy based purely on profit.

> A rise or fall in the prices of a number of leading articles is sufficient in the one case to increase, in the other to diminish, the sum of the prices of all commodities, and, therefore, to put more or less money in circulation. Whether the change in the price corresponds to an actual change of value in the commodities, or whether it be the result of mere fluctuations in market-prices, the effect on the quantity of the medium of circulation remains the same.[116]

The three factors which determine the market are: state of prices, quantity of circulating commodities, and velocity of money-currency. These factors "are all variable. Hence the sum of the prices to be realized, and consequently the quantity of the circulating medium depending on that sum, will vary with the numerous variations of these three factors."[117]

A slow historical process turns *money* into *capital*. As such, money gains a dynamic force and is no longer simply a means of payment, of spending, of saving or usury, not only a measure of value, but the *motive force of production.*

> The circulation of commodities is the starting-point of capital. The production of commodities, their circulation, and that more developed form of their circulation called commerce, these form the historical ground-work from which it rises. The modern history of capital dates from the creation in the sixteenth century of a world-embracing commerce and a world-embracing market.[118]

> The simple circulation of commodities—selling in order to buy—is a means of carrying out a purpose unconnected with circulation, namely, the appropriation of use-values, the satisfaction of wants. The circulation of money as capital is, on the contrary, an end in itself, for the expansion of value takes place only within this constantly renewed movement. The circulation of capital has therefore no limits.[119]

In simple commodity exchange the use-value predominates. Whoever sells his product wants to buy another with the money he has made. A demand for a concrete object is satisfied on both sides. But for the capitalist the object produced is a matter of indifference. He merely wants to turn his commodity, whatever it may be, into money. He wants to get more money out of it than he has put into it. The product

he sells must be so constituted that a part of the value that
has accrued to it through labor will fall into his hands.

> The expansion of value ... becomes his subjective aim, and it is only
> in so far as the appropriation of even more and more wealth in the
> abstract becomes the sole motive of his operations that he functions
> as a capitalist, that is, as capital personified and endowed with
> consciousness and a will. Use-values must therefore never be looked
> upon as the real aim of the capitalist; neither must the profit on any
> single transaction. The restless neverending process of profit-making
> alone is what he aims at. This boundless greed after riches, this
> passionate chase after exchange-value, is common to the capitalist
> and the miser; but while the miser is merely a capitalist gone mad,
> the capitalist is a rational miser. The never-ending augmentation of
> exchange-value, which the miser strives after by seeking to save his
> money from circulation, is attained by the more acute capitalist, by
> constantly throwing it afresh into circulation.[120]

How can the capitalist "expand" value and get more value
for himself in proportion as he puts more value on the market?
Occasionally he can do this by outwitting his fellow business-
men or as a result of price fluctuations and money speculation. But in the long run there must be some means that is
available to all capitalists, some commodity

> whose use-value possesses the peculiar property of being a source
> of value, whose actual consumption, therefore, is itself an embodi-
> ment of labor and, consequently, a creation of value. The possessor
> of money does find on the market such a special commodity in
> capacity for labor or labor-power.[121]

Labor-power

> can appear upon the market as a commodity, only if, and so far as,
> its possessor, the individual whose labor-power it is, offers it for sale,
> or sells it, as a commodity. In order that he may be able to do this,
> he must have it at his disposal, must be the untrammelled owner of
> his capacity for labor, i.e. of his person.... For the conversion of his
> money into capital, therefore, the owner of money must meet in the
> market with the free laborer, free in the double sense, that as a free
> man he can dispose of his labor-power as his own commodity, and
> that on the other hand he has no other commodity for sale, is short
> of everything necessary for the realization of his labor-power.[122]

This peculiar commodity, labor-power, has its value like all
other commodities. But how is this value determined?

> The value of labor-power is determined, as in the case of every other
> commodity, by the labor-time necessary for the production, and
> consequently also the reproduction, of this special article. So far as
> it has value, it represents no more than a definite quantity of the

average labor of society incorporated in it.... Given the individual, the production of labor-power consists in his reproduction of himself or his maintenance. For his maintenance he requires a given quantity of the means of subsistence. Therefore the labor-time requisite for the production of labor-power reduces itself to that necessary for the production of those means of subsistence; in other words, the value of labor-power is the value of the means of subsistence necessary for the maintenance of the laborer.[123]

The minimum limit of the value of labor-power is determined by the value of the commodities, without the daily supply of which the laborer cannot renew his vital energy, consequently by the value of those means of subsistence that are physically indispensable. If the price of labor-power falls to this minimum, it falls below its value, since under such circumstances it can be maintained and developed only in a crippled state. But the value of every commodity is determined by the labor-time requisite to turn it out so as to be of normal quality.

It is a very cheap sort of sentimentality which declares this method of determining the value of labor-power, a method prescribed by the very nature of the case, to be a brutal method.[124]

This rejection of cheap sentimentality, the hard matter-of-factness with which Marx speaks of labor-power as a commodity having a value and a price like any other, reveals more tellingly than any excess of feeling the viciousness of a system in which man is turned into a commodity like any dead product and the labor-time necessary for its reproduction becomes the value of that commodity. Marx, who was capable of such passion and pathos as an accuser, here does justice to the *dehumanization of man* in the world in which he lived by using the language of *objectification*.

Marx supposes that the value of a day's labor amounts to three shillings. Half a day's labor is embodied in that quantity of labor-power, because the means of subsistence that are daily required for the production of labor-power cost half a day's labor. But the past labor that is embodied in labor-power and the living labor that it can perform, the daily cost of maintaining labor-power and its own daily expenditure in work, are two totally different things. The former determines the exchange-value of labor-power, the latter its use-value.

The fact that half a day's labor is necessary to keep the laborer alive during twenty-four hours does not in any way prevent him from working a whole day. Therefore the value of labor-power, and the value which that labor-power creates in the labor-process, are two entirely different magnitudes; and this difference of the two values was what the capitalist had in view, when he was purchasing the labor-power....

Our capitalist foresaw this state of things, and that was the cause of his laughter. The laborer therefore finds, in the workshop, the means of production necessary for working, not only during six, but during twelve hours. Just as during the six hours' process our ten pounds of cotton absorbed six hours' labor, and became ten pounds of yarn, so now twenty pounds of cotton will absorb twelve hours' labor and be changed into twenty pounds of yarn. Let us now examine the product of this prolonged process. There is now materialized in this twenty pounds of yarn the labor of five days, of which four days are due to the cotton and the lost steel of the spindle, the remaining day having been absorbed by the cotton during the spinning process. Expressed in gold, the labor of five days is thirty shillings. This is therefore the price of the twenty pounds of yarn.... But the sum of the values of the commodities that entered into the process amounts to twenty-seven shillings. The value of the yarn is thirty shillings. Therefore the value of the product is one-ninth greater than the value advanced for its production; twenty-seven shillings have been transformed into thirty shillings; a surplus value of three shillings has been created.... Money has been converted into capital.[125]

To the usual objection that the capitalist also works and thereby contributes to the formation of value we may advance the question: What do capitalists live on whose only activity consists in cashing dividends? It is quite evident that workers, technicians, engineers and so forth perform *surplus labor*, a part of which becomes the revenue or income of one or several owners. If it were not for this surplus value the money the owners put in their pockets would have to be considered a free gift which the workers granted them out of pure Christian charity—a likely story!

True, the *product of labor* acquires part of its value from the *instrument of labor*, in which past labor is accumulated. What the product acquires, the instrument loses in terms of its use-value.

If such an instrument has no value to lose, if, in other words, it is not the product of human labor, it transfers no value to the product. It helps to create use-value without contributing to the formation of exchange-value. In this class are included all means of production supplied by Nature without human assistance, such as land, wind, water, metals in situ, and timber in virgin forests.[126]

... The means of production transfer value to the new product, so far only as during the labor-process they lose value in the shape of their old use-value. The maximum loss of value that they can suffer in the process is plainly limited by the amount of the original value with which they came into the process, or in other words, by the labor-time necessary for their production.[127]

The surplus of the total value of the product over the sum of values of its component elements (raw and auxiliary materials, instruments of labor and human labor-power) is thus obtained solely from the human labor-power which expends more labor-time than is necessary for its maintenance. That part of capital which is invested in the means of production does not change in value during the production process. Marx calls this *constant capital.*

> On the other hand, that part of capital, represented by labor-power, does, in the process of production, undergo an alteration of value. It both reproduces the equivalent of its own value, and also produces an excess, a surplus-value, which may itself vary, may be more or less according to circumstances. This part of capital is continually being transformed from a constant into a variable magnitude. I therefore call it the variable part of capital, or, shortly, *variable capital.*[128]

The labor-power which the worker expends beyond the labor necessary for his maintenance creates no value *for him.* It creates *surplus value*, which for the capitalist, as Marx puts it, "has all the charm of a creation out of nothing."[129]

The relationship between capitalist and worker presupposes a struggle from the outset: struggle for the *rate of surplus value*, i.e. the proportion of surplus labor-time to that labor-time necessary for the maintenance of labor-power—in other words, first and foremost, for the length of the working-day. The worker does not merely, like an animal, need a part of the day in order to rest, eat and satisfy his physical requirements.

> The laborer needs time for satisfying his intellectual and social wants, the extent and number of which are conditioned by the general state of social advancement. The variation of the working-day fluctuates, therefore, within physical and social bounds.[130]

What is a working-day? How much shorter should it be than a natural living day? The capitalist's view concerning the necessary limitation of the working-day differs from the worker's.

> As capitalist he is only capital personified.... But capital has one single life impulse, the tendency to create value and surplus-value,

to make its constant factor, the means of production, absorb the greatest possible amount of surplus-labor. Capital is dead labor, that, vampire-like, only lives by sucking living labor, and lives the more, the more labor it sucks. The time during which the laborer works, is the time during which the capitalist consumes the labor-power he has purchased of him. If the laborer consumes his disposable time for himself, he robs the capitalist.[131]

It would be quite wrong to imagine that Marx considered every capitalist to be a villain or a rogue. He did not see the capitalist as an individual but only as a "social character mask," a "functionary of capital," who, by virtue of the law of commodity exchange, demands the full value of the commodity he has purchased.

> The capitalist maintains his right as a purchaser when he tries to make the working-day as long as possible, and to make, whenever possible, two working-days out of one. On the other hand, the peculiar nature of the commodity sold implies a limit to its consumption by the purchaser, and the laborer maintains his right as seller when he wishes to reduce the working-day to one of definite normal duration. There is here, therefore, an antinomy, right against right, both equally bearing the seal of the law of exchanges. Between equal rights force decides. Hence is it that in the history of capitalist production, the determination of what is a working-day presents itself as the result of a struggle, a struggle between collective capital, i.e. the class of capitalists, and collective labor, i.e. the working class.[132]

With great matter-of-factness as well as passion, Marx described the progress of this struggle for the "normal working-day," particularly in England, as a struggle in which the laborers were able to win certain victories within the capitalist system, but in which, at the same time, they became aware of the limitations of that system based on the buying and selling of human labor-power—on surplus labor, not in the service of the community, but for private interest.

Finally, the fact that Marx foresaw the age of automation and, with it, the necessity to modify the theory of surplus value, testifies to his greatness as a thinker. In the *Grundrisse* he wrote:

> To the extent that large-scale industry is developed, the creation of real wealth comes to depend less and less on the labor time and the quantum of labor employed compared with the power of the agents set in motion during that labor time, which in its turn—in its *powerful effectiveness*—is not minimally related to the immediate labor time

that their production costs, but depends rather on the general state of science and of the progress of technology, or of the application of this science to production.... Work no longer seems to be included in the production process as man rather stands apart from the production process as its regulator and guardian.... He stands beside the production process rather than being its principal agent. In this transformation it is less the immediate labor performed by man himself or the time that he works than the appropriation of his general productivity, his comprehension of nature and dominion over it through his existence as a social body—in a word, the development of the social individual—that appears as the supporting pillar of production and wealth. The theft of the labor time of others on which wealth is based today appears as a miserable basis compared with the new basis which has developed in the meanwhile, created by a large-scale industry itself. Hardly has labor in an immediate form ceased to be the major source of wealth than labor time ceases, and must cease, to be its measure, and thus exchange-value the measure of use-value. The surplus labor of the masses has ceased to be the condition for the development of general wealth, just as the non-labor of the few has ceased to be the condition for the development of the general forces of the human mind. Thus production based on exchange-value crumbles....(*Marx's Notes on Machines*, translated by Ben Brewster, *Sublation* Offprint No. 1, Students' Union, Leicester University, 6 December 1966, pp. 14-16).

8
PROFIT AND CAPITAL

Capitalism is first and foremost a system for expanding the profits of capital. This, however, comes into conflict with the satisfaction of social needs and with the development of the means of production themselves. Overproduction crises beset capital due to the concentration of purchasing power (income and wealth) at the top of society, while redistribution strategies that would ameliorate this situation go against the primary character of the system—as a profit-making system geared to the accumulation of private wealth. At each point its advance production therefore finds itself threatened by the very limited class and property forms associated with the capitalist production mode. Consequently, recurrent economic crises are as much a part of capitalism as the search for profit itself.

Writing near the end of a quarter-century of prosperity in North America and Western Europe (from the end of World War II to 1970), Fischer found some agreement with those critics of Marx who argued that economic crises were no longer as great a problem for capitalism as in times past. The capitalist class was believed to have learned how to mitigate economic crisis through state demand-management—the Keynesian welfare state. Today, however, with capitalism again characterized by slow rates of growth, high levels of unemployment, and increasing global economic instability, and with the welfare state everywhere in decline, that very rethinking of Marxism needs to be rethought.—*JBF*

When value leaves the sphere of production, in which it originates, and enters that of the market, of commerce and circulation, it becomes price; as such, as we have seen, it also becomes more indefinite, more capricious, more readily influenced by a variety of circumstances. Value as price follows an adventurous course, especially when a sudden price drop reveals one of the secrets of the capitalist mode of production: namely, that production is, in principle, limitless and without measure, whereas consumption is limited by demand and purchasing power.

111

Something similar happens to *surplus value* when it leaves the sphere of production—in which alone it, too, has its origin—in order to reappear as *profit* in the sphere of the market, of distribution and sale. The cost-price of a commodity (i.e. the total sum expended on its production) is lower than its value. Commodity value = cost-price + profit.

> Hence, if a commodity is sold at its value, a profit is realized which is equal to the excess of its value over its cost-price, and therefore equal to the entire surplus-value incorporated in the value of the commodity. But the capitalist may sell a commodity at a profit even when he sells it below its value. So long as its selling-price is higher than its cost-price, though it may be lower than its value, a portion of the surplus-value incorporated in it is always realized, thus always yielding a profit. [133]

Marx dismisses as a "thoughtless conception" the idea that

> the cost-price of a commodity constitutes its actual value, and that surplus-value springs from selling the product above its value, so that commodities would be sold at their value if their selling-price were to equal their costing-price, i.e. if it were to equal the price of the consumed means of production plus wages. [134]

Surplus value is exclusively the result of living labor-power, of surplus labor, of the exploitation of the workers. The rate of surplus value—the proportion of surplus labor time to necessary labor time—therefore relates to variable capital only. Profit, on the other hand, relates to the total capital, both variable and constant. Hence the rate of profit is also the proportion of the sale price to the cost price.

> The rate of surplus-value measured against the variable capital is called rate of surplus-value. The rate of surplus-value measured against the total capital is called rate of profit. These are two different measurements of the same entity, and owing to the difference of the two standards of measurement they express different proportions or relations of this entity.
>
> The transformation of surplus-value into profit must be deduced from the transformation of the rate of surplus-value into the rate of profit, not vice versa. And in fact it was rate of profit which was the historical point of departure. Surplus-value and rate of surplus-value are, relatively, the invisible and unknown essence that wants investigating, while rate of profit and therefore the appearance of surplus-value in the form of profit are revealed on the surface of the phenomenon. [135]
>
> Although the rate of profit thus differs numerically from the rate of surplus-value, while surplus-value and profit are actually the same thing and numerically equal, profit is nevertheless a converted form

of surplus-value, a form in which its origin and the secret of its existence are obscured and extinguished. In effect, profit is the form in which surplus-value presents itself to the view, and must initially be stripped by analysis to disclose the latter. In surplus-value, the relation between capital and labor is laid bare; in the relation of capital to profit, i.e. of capital to surplus-value that appears on the one hand as an excess over the cost-price of commodities realized in the process of circulation and, on the other, as a surplus more closely determined by its relation to the total capital, the capital appears as a *relation to itself*, a relation in which it, as the original sum of value, is distinguished from a new value which it generated.[136]

The rate of profit is related to the rate of surplus-value as the variable capital is to the total capital.[137]

Thus the level of the rate of profit is dependent not only on that of the rate of surplus value, but also on the composition of the capital and its speed of circulation; but the fact that there can be profit at all is determined only by surplus labor, which creates surplus value. Although the two rates appear in different form, their intrinsic nature is the same.

As already pointed out,

Capitalist production is in itself indifferent to the particular use-value and distinctive features of any commodity it produces. In every sphere of production it is only concerned with producing surplus-value, and appropriating a certain quantity of unpaid labor incorporated in the product of labor.[138]

To the individual capitalist, however, the production process need by no means appear simply as a process of the production of surplus value. The capitalist may feel himself to be a captain of industry, not merely an exploiter of men. Besides being a "functionary of capital" obedient to the laws of capital, he may possess a distinct personality and may regard this fact as a decisive factor in the production process. The value of a commodity—profit—is *realized* in circulation: it may therefore appear as though it arose from it,

an appearance which is especially reinforced by two circumstances: first, the profit made in selling depends on cheating, deceit, inside knowledge, skill and a thousand favorable market opportunities; and then by the circumstance that added here to labor-time is a second determining element—time of circulation.[139]

Marx points out that rates of profit, although they differ between one enterprise and another, tend to approximate to an *average profit*, which individual capitalists are always trying to transcend by competitive struggle. "In fact, the direct interest taken by the capitalist, or the capital, of any individual sphere of production in the exploitation of the laborers who are directly employed is confined to making an extra gain, either through exceptional overwork, or reduction of the wage below the average, or through the exceptional productivity of the labor employed." But the most important fact is that the *total* capital is based on surplus value—profit—and is therefore interested in the exploitation of the workers, the varying degree of exploitation depending on the length of the working-day and the intensity of work.

A further tendency of the capitalist mode of production is that of the *fall in the rate of profit* simultaneous with the *growth of the mass of profit*. Capital invested in the instruments of labor (i.e. constant capital) grows with increasing production, whereas the ratio of variable to constant capital decreases.

The drive of capital towards ever-increasing production, constant expansion of value, and accumulation, the change in the relative proportions of constant and variable capital, the need for increasing exploitation as well as increasing consumption, the development of the productive power of labor so that more things are produced with the same capital and the same amount of work, and, lastly, the fall in the rate of profit all give rise to contradictory tendencies and phenomena until at last the profound contradiction inherent in capitalism can no longer be disguised.

> Alongside the fall in the rate of profit the mass of capital grows, and hand in hand with this there occurs a depreciation of existing capitals which checks the fall and gives an accelerating motion to the accumulation of capital-values.

> Alongside the development of productivity there develops a higher composition of capital, i.e. the relative decrease of the ratio of variable to constant capital.

> These different influences may at one time operate predominantly side by side in space, and at another succeed each other in time. From time to time the conflict of antagonistic agencies finds vent in crises. The crises are always but momentary and forcible solutions of the existing contradictions. They are violent eruptions which for a time restore the disturbed equilibrium.

> The contradiction, to put it in a very general way, consists in that the capitalist mode of production involves a tendency towards absolute development of the productive forces, regardless of the value and surplus-value it contains, and regardless of the social conditions under which capitalist production takes place; while, on the other

hand, its aim is to preserve the value limit (i.e. to promote an ever more rapid growth of this value).[140]

The tendency towards unrestrained production and unlimited development of the productive forces enters into contradiction with the maintenance of existing capital value.

Capitalist production seeks continually to overcome these immanent barriers, but overcomes them only by means which again place these barriers in its way and on a more formidable scale.

The *real barrier* of capitalist production is *capital itself.* It is that capital and its self-expansion appear as the starting and the closing point, the motive and the purpose of production; that production is only production for *capital* and not vice versa, the means of production are not mere means for a constant expansion of the living process of the *society* of producers. The limits within which the preservation or self-expansion of the value of capital resting on the expropriation and pauperization of the great mass of producers can alone move— these limits come continually into conflict with the methods of production employed by capital for its purposes, which drive towards unlimited extension of production, towards production as an end in itself, towards unconditional development of the social productivity of labor. The means—unconditional development of the productive forces of society—comes continually into conflict with the limited purpose, the self-expansion of the existing capital.[141]

With accumulation and concentration, capital's inherent tendency towards *over-production* is intensified. This, of course, does not mean over-production of *use-values*—the masses of mankind could do with many more of these—but of *exchange-values*, of commodities which cannot find a buyer.

Since the aim of capital is not to minister to certain wants, but to produce profit, and since it accomplishes this purpose by methods which adapt the mass of production to the scale of production, not *vice versa*, a rift must continually ensue between the limited dimensions of consumption under capitalism and a production which forever tends to exceed this immanent barrier. [142]

There are not too many necessities of life produced, in proportion to the existing population. Quite the reverse. Too little is produced to satisfy decently and humanely the wants of the great mass.

There are not too many means of production produced to employ the able-bodied portion of the population. Quite the reverse. In the first place, too large a portion of the produced population is not really capable of working, and is through force of circumstances made dependent on exploiting the labor of others, or on labor which can pass under this name only under a miserable mode of production. In the second place, not enough means of production are produced to permit the employment of the entire able-bodied population under the most productive conditions, so that their absolute working period could be shortened by the mass and effectiveness of the constant capital employed.

On the other hand, too many means of labor and necessities of life are produced at times to permit of their serving as means for the exploitation of laborers at a certain rate of profit. Too many commodities are produced to permit of a realization and conversion into new capital of the value and surplus-value contained in them under the conditions of distribution and consumption peculiar to capitalist production, i.e. too many to permit of the consummation of this process without constantly recurring explosions.

Not too much wealth is produced. But at times too much wealth is produced in its capitalistic, self-contradictory forms.

The limitations of the capitalist mode of production come to the surface:

(1) In that the development of the productivity of labor creates out of the falling rate of profit a law which at a certain point comes into antagonistic conflict with this development and must be overcome constantly through crises.

(2) In that the expansion or contraction of production are determined by the appropriation of unpaid labor and the proportion of this unpaid labor to materialized labor in general, or, to speak the language of the capitalists, by profit and the proportion of this profit to the employed capital, thus by a definite rate of profit, rather than the relation of production to social requirements, i.e. to the requirements of socially developed human beings....

The rate of profit is the motive power of capitalist production. Things are produced only so long as they can be produced with a profit. Hence the concern of the English economists over the decline of the rate of profit. The fact that the bare possibility of this happening should worry Ricardo, shows his profound understanding of the conditions of capitalist production. It is that which is held against him, it is his unconcern about "human beings," and his having an eye solely for the development of the productive forces, whatever the cost in human beings and capital-*values*—it is precisely that which is the most important thing about him. Development of the productive forces of social labor is the historical task and justification of capital. This is just the way in which it unconsciously creates the material requirements of a higher mode of production.[143]

This passage is doubly significant; it not only shows that Marx preferred the "cynicism" of bourgeois scientific economists to any sentimental obfuscation of real conditions, but also proves his historical objectivity. Marx was ruthless in unmasking the dehumanizing effects of capitalism; he passionately championed the working class and strove to develop its political consciousness; and yet he was also an objective historian who, while attacking a system, never overlooked its "historical task and justification." He described the origins of capital and its "primitive accumulation" with all its cruelties, but he also paid tribute to the historic role of capital. The chapter entitled "The So-Called Primitive Accumulation"[144] is one of the most magnificent and exciting passages in written history, and its content justifies the almost Shakespearean sentence: "If money, according to Augier,* 'comes into the world with a congenital blood-stain on one cheek,' capital comes dripping from head to foot, from every pore, with blood and dirt."[145]

Just as Marx saw *alienation* as the somber shadow cast upon the earth by the *division of labor*, while being able to affirm the division of labor as a stage in the development by which man progresses towards his full potential of humanity, so too he called for the struggle against capitalism in order to accelerate the transition—represented by capitalism—to higher social forms.

> Surplus-labor in general, as labor performed over and above the given requirement, must always remain.... It is one of the civilizing aspects of capital that it enforces this surplus-labor in a manner and under conditions which are more advantageous to the development of the productive forces, social relations, and the creation of the elements for a new and higher form than under the preceding forms of slavery, serfdom, etc. Thus it gives rise to a stage, on the one hand, in which coercion and monopolization of a social development (including its material and intellectual advantages) by one portion of society at the expense of the other are eliminated; on the other hand, it creates the material means and embryonic conditions, making it possible in a higher form of society to combine this surplus-labor with a greater reduction of time devoted to material labor in general.[146]

"The great historical aspect of capital," Marx wrote in the draft *Grundrisse*,

> is that it *creates surplus labor....* Capital as a ceaseless striving after the universal form of wealth drives labor beyond the confines of natural necessity and so creates the material element for the development of a rich individuality, which is as many-sided in its

---

* *Emile Augier* (1820-1889), French dramatist and author, a harsh critic of the social conditions of his time.

production as it is in its consumption. Thus the labor of this individuality will no longer appear as labor but as the full development of action itself, from which natural necessity in its immediate form has disappeared; because natural necessity has been replaced by historically created necessity. Therefore *capital is productive*, i.e. it is an essential relationship for the development of the social productive forces. It only ceases to be such where the development of these productive forces finds itself limited by capital.[147]

In every economic crisis the productive forces find themselves limited by capital. But the bourgeoisie has learned some lessons: it cannot break down the barrier, but it can push it farther back; it cannot avoid crises, but it can mitigate them. The unexampled growth of productive forces in our time has confronted the bourgeoisie with new problems, but it has also enriched it with new opportunities.

Marx assumed that *economic* crises would become increasingly acute, and in his time the assumption was well-founded. Despite the world economic crisis of 1929, history does not seem to have fulfilled his prediction. But the inner contradictions of the capitalist mode of production, which he analyzed, are today plainly to be seen by everyone, including non-Marxists; and *political* crises are indeed becoming more and more catastrophic.

9

THE PROBLEM OF
INCREASING MISERY

Did Marx adhere to a rigid, mechanical assertion that wages would gravitate toward physical subsistence levels—that they would always tend to drop to rock bottom? As Fischer points out in this chapter, Marx "never actually used the concept of a 'theory of increasing misery.'" For Marx the value of labor power was historically determined by custom, and by the "respective power of the combatants" in the class struggle. Real wages, he believed, would tend to increase slowly with accumulation but the growth of wages would lag behind the growth of income and wealth at the top of society. Over the long run, workers could expect to experience a declining relative share of income and wealth. On the other hand, Fischer challenges Marx's view (at least as it describes advanced economies in the 1960s) that an ever-growing industrial reserve army of the unemployed would overwhelm the attempts of workers to organize and maintain their wages within the system. By the 1990s, however, the rise of "downsizing" and the all-out attack on workers' rights have brought labor relations back to the bitterly harsh levels described by Marx.—JBF

For the young Marx the increasing misery of the worker was the inevitable result of his alienation. The product of the worker's labor confronts him as an alien, imperious commodity. Owning no means of production, he is thrust into the machinery of production by the stranger who owns them. He labors, not in order to satisfy a need, but because in the world of commodity production there is nothing else left for him to do. Therefore his misery increases, regardless of how high his wages are, in proportion with the volume and importance of his labor. The more wealth he produces, the poorer he becomes, whether his own wage rises or falls in the process. Higher wages do not confer human dignity upon the worker.

Marx, the author of *Capital*, was to remain faithful to this view. In Volume III of *Capital* (Chapter 5), Marx, now an old man, retraced the idea first outlined in the *Economic and Philosophic Manuscripts*. Between the two, it is true, lies the theory of value and surplus value, which placed the doctrine of increasing misery upon the foundations of a new political economy.

The production of surplus value is the chief object of capitalist production. Capital always seeks to extract more from the bone, nerve and brain of working-people, be it through the lengthening of the working-day, through intensification of work, or through increased productivity which has the effect of shortening that part of the working-day during which the worker produces a value corresponding to his wage and lengthening that part during which he performs unpaid labor for the capitalist. The capitalist must try, on pain of extinction, to increase productivity in order to resist competition. He must try to lower production costs in order temporarily to undercut his competitors. For this reason the capitalist has to accumulate part of the surplus value, add it to the existing capital, invest it in new machinery, etc. All methods of increasing surplus value are therefore methods of accumulation, and all methods of accumulation are methods of increasing surplus value.

> But all methods for the production of surplus-value are at the same time methods of accumulation; and every extension of accumulation becomes again a means for the development of these methods. It follows therefore that in proportion as capital accumulates, the lot of the laborer, be his payment high or low, must grow worse.[148]

The higher wages which workers can win by organized struggle, especially in periods of high employment (i.e. of minimum unemployment), only mean that the weight and strength of the golden chain is such that its tension can be slackened a little.

The worker's miserable condition lies first and foremost in the fact that by his labor he reproduces capital for the benefit of capital, and with it his own alienation and misery.

Capital, which is extremely economical with goods and machines, is recklessly extravagant with living men, with the flesh and blood, the nerve and brain of working-people; nothing is allowed to stand in the way of capital accumulation and increased profit.

> Hence Capital is reckless of the health or length of life of the laborer, unless under compulsion from society. To the outcry as to the physical and mental degradation, the premature death, the torture

of over-work, it answers: Ought these to trouble us since they increase our profits? But looking at things as a whole, all this does not, indeed, depend on the good or ill will of the individual capitalist. Free competition brings out the inherent laws of capitalist production, in the shape of external coercive laws having power over every individual capitalist.[149]

This ruthless chase after profit, the motive force of capitalist production, creates a continuous tendency towards the increasing misery of the workers; hence "the general tendency of capitalist production is not to raise, but to sink the average standard of wages" (*Wages, Price, and Profit*). The tendency is "modified" and restrained primarily by the workers themselves, who, especially in periods of high employment, are able to fight it and by doing so can "make the best of the occasional chances for their temporary improvement." But the tendency towards the increasing misery of the working class finds continuous expression in the lowering of the workers' relative share in the national income. This share, which is a share in the values produced by the workers themselves, diminishes constantly even in periods of rising wages, while the share of the capitalists increases, so that the workers, even with a rising income, can actually buy a constantly decreasing proportion of the products they have made.

Marx drew attention to several important factors in assessing the position of the working class, which must be taken into account when considering the question of the tendency towards increasing misery. These factors are threefold:

First and foremost there are economic crises, periodically recurrent in Marx's time, which largely cancel out any improvements in the standard of living of the workers and during which their increasing misery becomes patently evident in a number of ways, such as food and housing conditions, and, above all, mass unemployment.

Second, the effects of the intensification of labor, which is a form of lengthening of the working-day. In one hour of "concentrated" work more can be got out of the worker than in two "porous" hours; the worker can be forced to expend more than twice as much vital energy. Intensification of work means that the worker's living time is transformed to a still greater degree into labor time for the employer. As a result the worker is liable to age more quickly and becomes unable at an earlier age to keep pace with the working rhythms.

Lastly, the value of labor power (the means of subsistence necessary for the maintenance of the worker and his family) can increasingly be earned only by means of women and children working as well as the head of the family; his wage is no longer sufficient to ensure the maintenance and reproduction of the family and has to be supplemented and replaced by the family wage, the increase in the family income being always less than the increase in the total labor performed.

> The value of labor-power was determined, not only by the labor-time necessary to maintain the individual adult laborer, but also by that necessary to maintain his family. Machinery, by throwing every member of that family on to the labor-market, spreads the value of the man's labor-power over his whole family. It thus depreciates his labor-power. To purchase the labor-power of a family of four, workers may, perhaps, cost more than it formerly did to purchase the labor-power of the head of the family, but, in return, four days' labor takes the place of one, and their price falls in proportion to the excess of the surplus labor of four over the surplus-labor of one. In order that the family may live, four people must now, not only labor, but expend surplus-labor for the capitalist. Thus we see that machinery, while augmenting the human material that forms the principal object of capital's exploiting power, at the same time raises the degree of exploitation.[150]

Marx's investigation into the value of *labor power as a commodity* throws an important light on the concrete circumstances in which the capitalist tendency towards increasing misery of the working class is expressed. This value is determined by the value of the means of consumption which are necessary for the production, development and maintenance of a worker's labor power and the maintenance and reproduction of his family. As Marx points out in *Wages, Price, and Profit*, this value is made up of two elements: a physical one, determined by the means of consumption necessary for the maintenance and reproduction of labor power and representing the minimum limit of the value, and a historical and social one, the magnitude of which is determined by the class struggle and which is conditioned, in every country, by its particular standard of living and its traditions. In this respect wages take on the coloring of each particular civilization.

The specific social conditions under which men live and work give rise to specific needs whose satisfaction demands consumer goods beyond the minimum limit of the value of labor power. This historical and social element, which is capable of an infinite range of variations and is conditioned by the state of the productive forces, is decided by the class struggle.

> The fixation of its actual degree is only settled by the continuous struggle between capital and labor, the capitalist constantly tending to reduce wages to their physical minimum, and to extend the working day to its physical maximum, while the working man constantly presses in the opposite direction. The matter resolves itself into a question of the respective powers of the combatant.[151]

Here we encounter two factors which, in the sense that Marx used the term, "modify" the tendency towards increasing misery. Progressive technological development and increasing productivity lower the value of labor power by lowering the value of the goods required for its maintenance and reproduction. At the same time they alter social wants and create an automatic necessity to produce new consumer goods. Thus technical progress lowers the value of labor power on the one hand and, on the other hand, creates new demands and new goods as a natural part of that value. The position of the workers must always be measured by the value of labor power, which comprises, *inter alia*, this historical and social element of new demands created by production itself.

> A house may be large or small; as long as the surrounding houses are equally small it satisfies all social demands for a dwelling. But let a palace arise beside the little house, and it shrinks from a little house to a hut. The little house shows now that its owner has only very slight or no demands to make; and however high it may shoot up in the course of civilization, if the neighboring palace grows to an equal or even greater extent, the occupant of the relatively small house will feel more and more uncomfortable, dissatisfied, and cramped within its four walls.

> A noticeable increase in wages presupposes a rapid growth of productive capital. The rapid growth of productive capital brings about an equally rapid growth of wealth, luxury, social wants, social enjoyments. Thus, although the enjoyments of the worker have risen, the social satisfaction that they give has fallen in comparison with the increased enjoyments of the capitalist, which are inaccessible to the worker, in comparison with the state of development of society in general. Our desires and pleasures spring from society; we measure them, therefore, by society and not by the objects which serve for their satisfaction. Because they are of a social nature, they are of a relative nature.[152]

The second decisive counter-tendency to production for production's sake and the consequent deterioration of the condition of the workers was, Marx thought, the battle fought by the workers themselves. Marx attached great importance to the struggle of the trade unions. At the same time, he believed that what he called the "general law of capitalist accumulation" set certain fixed limits upon the workers' struggle for improved conditions of life.

The composition of capital changes with accumulation. The portion spent on machinery, construction, raw materials, etc., rises compared with that spent on wages. The latter may increase absolutely, but it is bound to diminish compared with the other part of capital. Hence a part of the labor force is always made redundant by capital accumulation. A relative surplus-population is created—the so-called "industrial reserve army," displaced by machines and technology—which, especially in periods of crisis, separates out a "lazarus-layer" of the most wretched paupers, and which constantly depresses the wage level of the employed.

> *This is the absolute general law of capitalist accumulation.* Like all other laws it is modified in its working by many circumstances....[153]

> It establishes an accumulation of misery corresponding with accumulation of capital. Accumulation of wealth at one pole is, therefore, at the same time accumulation of misery, agony of toil, slavery, ignorance, brutality, mental degradation at the opposite pole, i.e. on the side of the class that produces its own product in the form of capital.[154]

The antagonistic character of capitalist production, that is to say the irreconcilable class antagonism between capital and labor, finds its clearest and most brutal expression in times of economic crises. But the law applies to all periods of capitalist production and depresses the situation of the worker, "be his payment high or low," at all times.

Unlike his critics and some of his disciples, Marx never actually used the concept of a "theory of increasing misery." But the general law of capitalist accumulation does represent a theory of increasing misery, since it is obvious that Marx did not regard the workers' struggle as an adequate counter-tendency to the continuous formation of industrial reserve armies and the simultaneous declassing of layers of the proletariat. In this respect Marx has been proved wrong, at least so far as the workers in the advanced capitalist countries are concerned. But in the global sense his broad historical vision proved correct when he pointed out that in assessing the situation of workers it was necessary to consider the world market as a whole, and that the wages of some could rise only because others were starving.

10
THE THEORY OF REVOLUTION

According to Marx, the contradiction that develops within any given class society, between the developing productive forces and the existing property forms, constitutes the key to instability and revolutionary change. Thus the rise and fall of the ancient and feudal modes of production and the development of the capitalist mode could all be understood in these terms. The most visible sign of this contradiction under capitalism was to be found in "the epidemics of overproduction" and economic crisis, bringing into bold relief the incompatibility between the social character of production and the system of private appropriation. Marx originally thought that revolutions against capitalism would arise within the most developed capitalist countries, such as Britain, France, and Germany. Late in his life, however, he looked to less developed countries on the periphery of the capitalist world, particularly Russia, which he hoped would serve as a detonator for revolution within the core of the system. This pointed toward the idea, widespread in the twentieth century, that the system would tend to break down at its weakest links, in the underdeveloped or "backward" nations.—*JBF*

The theory of revolution is the consequence and the concentrated expression of Marx's view of historical development, that is to say of the sequence of social formations in history. In their struggle for a living, in their dialogue with nature, men develop certain instruments, tools, forms of labor, and experiences which Marx described as productive forces; and he described as production relations the relations governing men's existence, which are essentially dependent on who owns the means of production. He saw the driving force of social development in the historical tendency towards establishing production relations (or property relations) which correspond to the level of development and the character of the productive forces at any time. In this "law of motion of history"—always activated by social groups, classes whose interests coincide with the developing tendency—he saw the key to understanding the sequence of the various forms of social order (primitive communism, slavery, feudalism, capitalism), though not quite according to the simple linear scheme later to be drawn in various textbooks of Marxism. On the evidence of the transition from feudalism to capitalism, of bourgeois revolutions, one might say of Western European history in general, he methodically and concretely modified the law of historical motion, and with it the theory of socialist revolution. Nevertheless, in the already quoted *Preface to a Contribution to the Critique of Political Economy* he expanded the particular to the general.

> In the social production of their life, men enter into definite relations that are indispensable and independent of their will, relations of production which correspond to a definite stage of development of their material productive forces.... At a certain stage of their development the material productive forces of society come in conflict with the existing relations of production, or—what is but a legal expression for the same thing—with the property relations within which they have been at work hitherto. From forms of development of the productive forces these relations turn into their fetters. Then begins an epoch of social revolution.[155]

Wherein did Marx see the conflict between productive forces and production relations which leads to socialist revolution?

The development of productive forces under capitalism extends their social character, and this finds expression in the creation of major enterprises, the increasing coordination of labor processes, the intermingling of production processes and the dominant role of industrial production in society as a whole. Capitalist ownership of the means of production and capitalist appropriation of the product become, at a certain point, fetters on the development of the productive forces; this is particularly evident in the periodically recurring crises which, Marx assumed both in the *Communist Manifesto* and in *Capital*, would become continually more violent and all-embracing. In these "epidemics of overproduction" the social character of production revolts against capitalist property relations. The social character of production demands social ownership of the means of production.

Economic crises bring this conflict into the open. "The ultimate reason for all real crises always remains the poverty and restricted consumption of the masses as opposed to the drive of capitalist production to develop the productive forces as though only the absolute consuming power of society constituted their limit."[156]

Let us recall once more the passage in *Capital* which we have already quoted:

> The monopoly of capital becomes a fetter upon the mode of production, which has sprung up and flourished along with, and under it. Centralization of the means of production and socialization of labor at last reach a point where they become incompatible with their capitalist integument. This integument is burst asunder. The knell of capitalist private property sounds. The expropriators are expropriated.[157]

The *Communist Manifesto*, twenty years earlier, had already drawn the comparison with the bourgeois revolution:

> At a certain stage in the development of these means of production and of exchange, the conditions under which feudal society produced and exchanged, the feudal organization of agriculture and manufacturing industry, in one word, the feudal relations of property became no longer compatible with the already developed productive forces; they became so many fetters. They had to be burst asunder; they were burst asunder.
>
> Into their place stepped free competition, accompanied by a social and political constitution adapted to it, and by the economic and political sway of the bourgeois class.
>
> A similar movement is going on before our own eyes. Modern bourgeois society with its relations of production, of exchange and of property, a society that has conjured up such gigantic means of production and of exchange, is like the sorcerer, who is no longer able to control the powers of the nether world whom he has called up by his spells. For many a decade past the history of industry and commerce is but the history of the revolt of modern productive forces against modern conditions of production, against the property relations that are the conditions for the existence of the bourgeoisie and of its rule.[158]

But the transition to socialism does not take place automatically. It is enforced by the revolution of the working class, for this class, itself "the greatest productive force," suffers more than any other from the conflict between productive forces and production relations. Since under capitalism there is production only as long as there is profit, the socialization of the means of production is the special interest of the working class. It has only "to set free the elements of the new society with which old collapsing bourgeois society itself is pregnant."[159]

The notion that the social character of the productive forces is already pressing for recognition within capitalist society and seeking to establish forms of property and production compatible with itself is an important one which has often been overlooked in later exposés of Marxist doctrine. At first Marx believed that stock companies were an expression of the incompatibility between the volume of the means of production and private property:

> The capital, which in itself rests on a social mode of production and presupposes a social concentration of means of production and labor-power, is here directly endowed with the form of social capital (capital of directly associated individuals) as distinct from private capital, and its undertakings assume the form of social undertakings as distinct from private undertakings. It is the abolition of capital as private property within the framework of capitalist production itself.[160]

> This result of the ultimate development of capitalist production is a necessary transitional phase towards the reconversion of capital into the property of producers, although no longer as the private property of the individual producers, but rather as the property of associated producers, as outright social property. On the other hand, the stock company is a transition towards the conversion of all functions in the reproduction process which still remain linked with capitalist property, into mere functions of associated producers, into social functions.[161]

Marx regarded this process, which later led to the formation of monopolies and trusts and culminated in forms of state ownership, as being related to a partial recognition by the capitalists of the social character of the productive forces. He saw the process as evidence that the capitalist had forfeited his function, a fact also confirmed by the increasing separation between ownership and administrative control—the administration of enterprises being taken over more and more by "managers" (Marx already employed this term). In a historical sense the capitalist owner had lost his function, and the working class, again in a historical sense, had the task of openly appropriating the means of production on behalf of society and, by socializing the means of production, assisting the increasingly evident social character of production to assert itself.

This being so, it is natural that Marx should have expected the social revolution to occur more or less simultaneously in the developed countries of Western Europe, and most probably first in the most industrially developed country—England.

Superb diagnostician though Marx was, history failed to confirm this prognosis. The means of production were first socialized in backward countries—a historical fact which accounts for the central problems of Marxism and the labor movement today. Yet it is interesting and significant from the viewpoint of the later development of Marxism and the labor movement that backward countries can temporarily move into the forefront of revolutionary development and that the unresolved problems of the bourgeois revolution can act as detonators for a transition to the socialist revolution. Already in the *Communist Manifesto* we read the following highly significant passage:

> The Communists turn their attention chiefly to Germany, because that country is on the eve of a bourgeois revolution that is bound to be carried out under more advanced conditions of European civilization, and with a much more developed proletariat, than that of England was in the seventeenth, and of France in the eighteenth century, and because the bourgeois revolution in Germany will be but the prelude to an immediately following proletarian revolution.[162]

This doubtless represented a certain revision of the "law of motion." To put it crudely, it meant that the backwardness of a country could prove beneficial to revolutionary perspectives, the unused reserves of the bourgeois revolution acting as fuel for the socialist revolution. Marx persisted in this view after the collapse of the revolution of 1848 in Germany, but with the subtle difference that he allotted to the petty-bourgeois democrats the role of leaders of a bourgeois revolution. This revolution would content itself with social reforms, and it was the task of the working class to develop it into a socialist revolution reaching beyond the frontiers of Germany. In the *Address of the Central Committee to the Communist League* of March 1850 we read:

> While the democratic petty bourgeois wish to bring the revolution to a conclusion as quickly as possible, and with the achievement, at most, of the above demands, it is our interest and our task to make the revolution permanent, until all more or less possessing classes have been forced out of their position of dominance, until the proletariat has conquered state power, and the association of proletarians, not only in one country but in all the dominant countries of the world, has advanced so far that competition among the proletarians of these countries has ceased and that at least the decisive productive forces are concentrated in the hands of the proletarians....

> If the German workers are not able to attain power and achieve their own class interests without completely going through a lengthy

> revolutionary development, they at least know for a certainty this time that the first act of this approaching revolutionary drama will coincide with the direct victory of their own class in France and will be very much accelerated by it...
>
> Their battle cry must be: The Revolution in Permanence.[163]

This document later gained great importance in the argument on "permanent revolution" within the Bolshevik party, an argument that was to have extremely grave consequences. But even in the 1880s Marx was already "turning his attention chiefly" to Russia, because there, "with a much more developed proletariat than that of England in the seventeenth and France in the eighteenth century"—and in some respects than that of Germany of the 1840s—the bourgeois revolution was the order of the day. The preface to the Russian edition of the *Communist Manifesto* in 1882 named Russia as "the vanguard of revolutionary action in Europe" and even spoke of the possibility that the Russian village community might pass directly to communist common ownership. But Russia, the backward country—like Germany forty years previously—was allotted the role of initial detonator destined to touch off a socialist revolution, whose actual arena would be in developed Western Europe:

> If the Russian Revolution becomes the signal for a proletarian revolution in the West, so that both complement each other, the present Russian common ownership of land may serve as the starting point for a communist development.[164]

Marx saw the essential content of the socialist revolution in the transfer of the means of production into public ownership, a process which was to take place under the leadership of the working class as having a greater interest in it than any other class. The question of the form in which this process was to occur—by peaceful or violent means—was for Marx a secondary issue, and his attitude towards it differed considerably at different times. Generally speaking, the older Marx remained faithful to the young Marx's view that violence is *midwife* to every society pregnant with a new one: but he never maintained that violence *begets* the new society. Thus it was not a fundamental inconsistency when he wrote in *The Poverty of Philosophy*, the *Communist Manifesto*, and other works that the rule of the proletariat could be founded only on the forcible overthrow of the bourgeoisie, or, in a letter to his friend

Kugelmann in 1871, that it was essential for every real people's revolution on the continent to "smash" the machinery of the State—while at the same time speaking of the possibility of a peaceful revolution in America, England, and Holland. He oriented the members of the International towards both possibilities:

> We must declare to the governments: we know that you are the armed power which is directed against the proletariat; we shall proceed against you by peaceful means where possible, and by force of arms if necessary.[165]

11

DICTATORSHIP OF THE PROLETARIAT, SOCIALISM, COMMUNISM

It is often assumed that Marx's notion of the transition to a socialist or communist society involved the glorification of state power; that all he envisioned was a transfer of the old state power to the victorious proletariat. In fact, Marx's theory of society was rooted in a critique of political alienation and state repression. The goal of the proletariat, he insisted, must be to seize the state in order to transform it. He proposed the elimination the state altogether, replacing its historic form as a means of repression with the "dictatorship of the proletariat," envisioned as a transitory democratic state implanted to defend the embattled revolutionary government. As the need for emergency measures associated with a new government and power arrangement subsided, Marx postulated, the path to communism—a society in which the free association of productive humanity overcomes both the power of the state and the "divine right" of concentrated ownership—would be opened.—*JBF*

Going beyond Hegel's conception of the State, the young Marx analyzed the State as a political expression of human alienation, an instrument, created by men, which had made itself independent and was turned against its creators. Marx always remained faithful to this interpretation, viewing the state apparatus as a product—alienated from the society which produced it. This apparatus, Marx believed, serves the ruling classes, but also acquires a certain independence, especially in situations where the classes are in temporary equilibrium. Its tendency towards autonomy grows stronger in such situations and results in phenomena such as Bonapartism, when a dictator supported by the state apparatus can appoint himself the guardian of the nation. Marx believed that one of the principal tasks of the socialist revolution was to overcome this political alienation, this alienated political power.

"The working class," Marx wrote in *The Poverty of Philosophy*,

> in the course of its development, will substitute for the old civil society an association which will exclude classes and their antagonism, and there will be no more political power properly so-called, since political power is precisely the official expression of antagonism in civil society.[166]

In *The Poverty of Philosophy*, civil war appears as a precondition of this goal, as it does in the *Communist Manifesto* a year later, where Marx's ideas concerning the forms of revolution and the tasks of the victorious proletariat are stated more precisely:

> In depicting the most general phases of the development of the proletariat we traced the more or less veiled civil war, raging within existing society, up to the point where that war breaks out into open revolution, and where the violent overthrow of the bourgeoisie lays the foundation for the sway of the proletariat....

> We have seen above that the first step in the revolution by the working class is to raise the proletariat to the position of ruling class, to win the battle of democracy.

> The proletariat will use its political supremacy to wrest, by degrees, all capital from the bourgeoisie, to centralize all instruments of production in the hands of the State, i.e. of the proletariat organized as the ruling class; and to increase the total of productive forces as rapidly as possible.[167]

With this idea, too, Marx kept faith all his life. The elevation of the proletariat to the position of a ruling class, the establishment of a state under the leadership of the working class—for which French socialists of the period employed the term "dictatorship of the proletariat"—means the achievement of democracy, the creation of conditions which render it possible to transfer the means of production into public ownership. The state which comes into being as a result of violent struggle against the exploiting classes is a state under the leadership of the victorious proletariat, the majority of the people, and in that sense, therefore, a democratic state. The *Manifesto* makes no mention of the complete abolition of state power, but this vision remains inherent in Marx's concept of the state.

We have already said that Marx modified the law of motion of history and with it the socialist revolution, principally of the transition from feudalism to capitalism, that is to say of

Western European history. The theory of the socialist revolution was largely influenced by the experience of the three French Revolutions of 1789, 1830, and 1848. The concept of the State was largely conditioned by the analysis of the French state, on the basis of the experience of the Revolution of 1848 and the *coup d'état* of Napoleon III. It seemed more than ever necessary to Marx to smash the rigidly organized state apparatus in order to leave the way free for a development that would lead via the rule of the proletariat to the abolition of all state power; and this seemed possible only in the aftermath of a civil war. Marx retained this conviction, so far as France was concerned, even at a time when he allowed for the possibility of a peaceful development in England, America, and Holland, where the state apparatus had not at that time attained the centralized power it had in France. We should recall that eight years After Marx's death Engels regarded this possibility as conceivable for France too.

However, in *The Eighteenth Brumaire of Louis Bonaparte* the statement is unequivocal:

> But the revolution is thoroughgoing. It is still journeying through purgatory. It does its work methodically. By December 2, 1851 it had completed one half of its preparatory work; it is now completing the other half. First it perfected the parliamentary power, in order to be able to overthrow it. Now that it has attained this, it perfects the *executive power*, reduces it to its purest expression, isolates it, sets it up against itself as the sole target, in order to concentrate all its forces of destruction against it. And when it has done this second half of its preliminary work, Europe will leap from its seat and exultantly exclaim: Well grubbed, old mole!

> This executive power with its enormous bureaucratic and military organization, with its ingenious state machinery, embracing wide strata, with a host of officials numbering half a million, besides an army of another half million, this appalling parasitic body, which enmeshes the body of French society like a net and chokes all its pores, sprang up in the days of the absolute monarchy, with the decay of the feudal system, which it helped to hasten.... The first French Revolution ... developed ... centralization, but at the same time the extent, the attributes and the agents of governmental power. Napoleon perfected this state machinery. The Legitimist monarchy and the July monarchy added nothing but a greater division of labor.... Finally ... the parliamentary republic found itself compelled to strengthen, along with the repressive measures, the resources and centralization of governmental power. All revolutions perfected this machine instead of smashing it. The parties that contended in turn for domination regarded the

possession of this huge state edifice as the principal spoils of the victor.[168]

For the state to be created after the smashing of the centralist, parasitic state apparatus, a state led by the working class and gradually socializing the means of production, Marx took over the concept of the "dictatorship of the proletariat." Within this concept was implicit the vision of grand and violent struggles and victories, but also of increasing democracy for the masses of the population. Marx wrote to his friend Josef Weydemeyer on March 5, 1852:

> And now as to myself, no credit is due to me for discovering the existence of classes in modern society, nor yet the struggle between them. Long before me bourgeois historians had described the historical development of this struggle of the classes and bourgeois economists the economic anatomy of the classes. What I did that was new was to prove: (1) that the *existence of classes* is only bound up with *particular historical phases in the development of production*; (2) that the class struggle necessarily leads to the *dictatorship of the proletariat*; (3) that this dictatorship itself only constitutes the transition to the *abolition of all classes* and to a *classless society*.[169]

Marx's concept of the state, then, was modified in the light of the events in France from 1848 to 1852. His view of a new state under the leadership of the working class—the state of the socialist revolution, and the functions of such a state—was modified and made concrete by the example of the Paris Commune of 1871. He regarded the short-lived Paris Commune as the first form of a workers' government, which by its practical actions and the measures it adopted had proved that the transition to socialism is bound up with a fundamentally new state system. Such a state system is no longer a state in the old sense of the word, because, after the smashing of the old state apparatus, it develops forms of popular control over the executive and the bureaucracy which correspond to the vision of the abolition of all central political power. We read in *The Civil War in France*, which appeared directly after the defeat of the Paris Commune, that the nineteenth century saw the development of "centralized State power, with its ubiquitous organs of standing army, police, bureaucracy, clergy, and judicature"—a power whose origins went back to the Middle Ages. With the intensification of class antagonism between capital and labor

> the State power assumed more and more the character of the national power of capital over labor, of a public force organized for social enslavement, of an engine of class despotism. After every revolution

marking a progressive phase in the class struggle, the purely repressive character of the State power stands out in bolder and bolder relief.

After the revolution of 1848, State power became "the national war-engine of capital against labor." The Second Empire reinforced this state of affairs.

"The direct antithesis of the empire was the Commune." The Commune was the distinct form of "a Republic that was not to supersede the monarchical form of class-rule, but class-rule itself."

"The first decree of the Commune ... was the suppression of the standing army, and the substitution for it of the armed people."

> The Commune was formed of the municipal councillors, chosen by universal suffrage in the various wards of the town, responsible and revocable at short terms. The majority of its members were naturally working men, or acknowledged representatives of the working class.... Instead of continuing to be the agent of the Central Government, the police was at once stripped of its political attributes, and turned into the responsible and at all times revocable agent of the Commune. So were the officials of all other branches of the Administration. From the members of the Commune downwards the public service had to be done at *workmen's wages*. The vested interests and the representation allowances of the high dignitaries of State disappeared along with the high dignitaries themselves.... The judicial functionaries were to be divested of that sham independence which had but served to mask their abject subservience to all succeeding governments ... magistrates and judges were to be elective, responsible, and revocable.

Eight years after Marx's death Frederick Engels described these fundamental features of the new state form in an introduction to the third edition of *The Civil War in France*, as follows:

> It was precisely the oppressing power of the former centralized government, army, political police, bureaucracy, which Napoleon had created and which since then had been taken over by every new government as a welcome instrument and used against its opponents—it was precisely this power which was to fall everywhere, just as it had already fallen in Paris.

> From the very outset the Commune was compelled to recognize that the working class, once come to power, could not go on managing with the old state machine; that in order not to lose again its only just conquered supremacy, this working class must, on the one hand, do away with all the old repressive machinery previously used against it itself, and, on the other, safeguard itself against its own deputies

and officials, by declaring them all, without exception, subject to recall at any moment....

Against this transformation of the state and the organs of the state from servants of society into masters of society—an inevitable transformation in all previous states—the Commune made use of two infallible means. In the first place, it filled all posts—administrative, judicial and educational—by election on the basis of universal suffrage of all concerned, subject to the right of recall at any time by the same electors. And, in the second place, all officials, high or low, were paid only the wages received by other workers. The highest salary paid by the Commune to anyone was 6,000 francs. In this way an effective barrier to place-hunting and careerism was set up, even apart from the binding mandates to delegates to representative bodies which were added besides....

The Commune was to be a working, not a parliamentary, body, executive and legislative at the same time....

Instead of deciding once in three or six years which member of the ruling class was to misrepresent the people in Parliament, universal suffrage was to serve the people, constituted in Communes, as individual suffrage serves every other employer in the search for the workmen and managers in his business.[170]

Control from below, democracy spreading from below to the top, the democratic abolition of political alienation as he had described it in his youth—in these features lay the significance of the Paris Commune for Marx. He saw them as vitally important for the socialist states to come, for future dictatorships of the proletariat operating "as the transition to the abolition of classes and with them of the state."[171]

"In a rough sketch of national self-government which the Commune had no time to develop, it states clearly that the Commune was to be the political form of even the smallest country hamlet." The Communes, too, were to elect deputies to the National Delegation in Paris:

The few but important functions which still would remain for a central government were not to be suppressed, as has been intentionally mis-stated, but were to be discharged by Communal, and therefore strictly responsible agents. The unity of the nation was not to be broken, but, on the contrary, to be organized by the Communal Constitution, and to become a reality by the destruction of the State power which claimed to be the embodiment of that unity independent of, and superior to, the nation itself, from which it was but a parasitic excrescence. While the merely repressive organs of the old governmental power were to be amputated, its legitimate functions were to be wrested from an authority usurping pre-eminence over society itself, and restored to the responsible agents of society.

The Communal Constitution would have restored to the social body all the forces hitherto absorbed by the State parasite feeding upon, and clogging the free movement of, society. By this one act it would have initiated the regeneration of France....

In reality, the Communal Constitution brought the rural producers under the intellectual lead of the central towns of their districts, and there secured to them, in the working men, the natural trustees of their interests. The very existence of the Commune involved, as a matter of course, local municipal liberty, but no longer as a check upon the, now superseded, State power....

The multiplicity of interpretations to which the Commune has been subjected, and multiplicity of interests which construed it in their favor, show that it was a thoroughly expansive political form, while all previous forms of government had been emphatically repressive. Its true secret was this. It was essentially a working-class government, the product of the struggle of the producing against the appropriating class, the political form at last discovered under which to work out the economic emancipation of labor.

Except on this last condition, the Communal Constitution would have been an impossibility and a delusion.[172]

It is within this meaning of a "dictatorship of the proletariat" that we should understand Marx's celebrated dictum in the *Critique of the Gotha Programme*, written four years after the Paris Commune:

Between capitalist and communist society lies the period of the revolutionary transformation of the one into the other. There corresponds to this also a political transition period in which the state can be nothing but the *revolutionary dictatorship of the proletariat*.[173]

In this work Marx distinguishes two phases in the development of communist society, the first or lower phase when it is still "stamped with the birthmarks of the old society from whose womb it emerges" and when it distributes the available consumer goods according to the principle of performance, and the second phase—Communism—in which the sources of production are already flowing so abundantly that to each may be given according to his needs:

With an equal performance of labor and hence an equal share in the social consumption fund, one will in fact receive more than another, one will be richer than another, and so on. To avoid all these defects, right instead of being equal would have to be unequal.

But these defects are inevitable in the first phase of communist society as it is when it has just emerged after prolonged birth pangs from capitalist society. Right can never be higher than the economic structure of society and its cultural development conditioned thereby.

In a higher phase of communist society, after the enslaving subordination of the individual to the division of labor, and therewith also the antithesis between mental and physical labor, has vanished; after the productive forces have also increased with the all-round development of the individual, and all the springs of cooperative wealth flow more abundantly—only then can the narrow horizon of bourgeois right be crossed in its entirety and society inscribe on its banners: From each according to his ability, to each according to his needs![174]

From the context of Marx's whole body of ideas it emerges with certainty that he imagined the victory of the revolution and of socialism as a more or less simultaneous process in the advanced capitalist countries, and that the social order he had before his mind's eye was the one of which the *Communist Manifesto* had said: "...the free development of each is the condition for the free development of all."

12

LABOR MOVEMENT AND INTERNATIONAL

A widespread myth holds that, from the beginning of his exile in London in 1849, Marx had no direct connection to revolutionary politics and was merely an isolated scholar working in the British Museum. This is contradicted by Marx's role as the leading figure in the International Working Men's Association (also known as the First International) from its founding in 1864 to its demise in 1873. It is in this context that Marx left an invaluable legacy of political organization, embodying principles relevant to our time. As Fischer emphasizes, this legacy included a struggle against sectarianism within the working class movement, i.e. the separation of certain sects from the actual, unfolding struggles of workers in general, based on notions of political purity. Thus Marx insisted on the importance of supporting workers' efforts to improve their conditions, socially, politically, and economically, through trade unions, labor protection laws, etc. In the struggles of workers, Marx drew attention to a "political economy of the working class," opposed to "the political economy of capital" and pointing beyond the logic of present-day society.—*JBF*

As part of his theory of revolution and his concept of theory, Marx saw the proletariat as the social force destined, because of its position within the production process and within history, to accomplish the transition to the socialist way of life—not because workers are gods, but because the inhumanity of capitalist society assumes its most concentrated form in the conditions of their life. In *The Holy Family* the young Marx wrote:

> The proletariat executes the sentence that private property pronounced on itself by begetting the proletariat, just as it carries out the sentence that wage-labor pronounced on itself by bringing forth wealth for others and misery for itself....
>
> When socialist writers ascribe this historic role to the proletariat, it is not, as Critical Criticism pretends to think, because they consider

the proletarians as *gods*. Rather the contrary. Since the abstraction of all humanity, even of the *semblance* of humanity, is practically complete in the full-grown proletariat; since the conditions of life of the proletariat sum up all the conditions of life of society today in all their inhuman acuity; since man has lost himself in the proletariat, yet at the same time has not only gained theoretical consciousness of that loss, but through urgent, no longer disguisable, absolutely imperative need—that practical expression of *necessity*—is driven directly to revolt against that inhumanity; it follows that the proletariat can and must free itself. But it cannot free itself without abolishing the conditions of its own life. It cannot abolish the conditions of its own life without abolishing *all* the inhuman conditions of life of society today which are summed up in its own situation. Not in vain does it go through the stern but steeling school of *labor*. The question is not what this or that proletarian, or even the whole of the proletariat at the moment *considers* as its aim. The question is *what the proletariat is*, and what, consequent on that *being*, it will be compelled to do. Its aim and historical action is irrevocably and obviously demonstrated in its own life situation as well as in the whole organization of bourgeois society today.[175]

Marx never hesitated to attack narrow craft attitudes within the labor movement and to uphold the necessity for a scientific understanding of social conditions as a basis for political action. Concerning the "League of the Just" (from which originated the Communist League on whose behalf Marx and Engels composed the *Communist Manifesto*), he once wrote that "scientific insight into the economic structure of bourgeois society" had to be established as the "only tenable theoretical basis," and an explanation in popular form had to be given that "we are not concerned with imposing some utopian system, but with self-conscious participation in the historical process of revolutionizing society, which is taking place before our eyes."[176]

Marx emphasized this concept of a realistic, scientifically founded labor policy after the defeat of the revolution of 1848 when, as often happens after the failure of a revolutionary movement, actions and initiatives of all kinds were being proposed within the League of Communists in order to avoid having to face the reality of the situation. At a meeting held on September 15, 1850, when a split in the League occurred, Marx described the opposing attitudes in the following terms:

> The minority puts a dogmatic view in place of the critical, and an idealist one in place of the materialist. They regard mere discontent, instead of real conditions, as the driving wheel of revolution. Whereas we tell the workers: You have to go through fifteen, twenty, fifty years of civil wars and national struggles, not only in order to change conditions but also to change yourselves and make yourself capable of political rule; you, on the contrary, say: "We must come to power immediately, or else we may as well go to sleep." Whilst we make a special point of directing the German workers' attention to the undeveloped state of the German proletariat, you flatter the national feeling and the status-prejudice of the German artisans in the crudest possible way—which, admittedly, is more popular. Just as the word "people" has been made holy by the democrats, so the word "proletariat" has been made holy by you.[177]

For more than a decade Marx regarded his and Engels's writings and scientific studies as the decisive activity on behalf of the Party—the Party not in the narrow but in the historical sense.

Marx re-entered the political labor movement only when "real forces" were once again in play. At the foundation meeting of the Working Men's International Association (First International) on September 28, 1864, he at first sat in silence on the tribune; later the meeting invited him to compose its "inaugural address" and in that way he became its intellectual leader. He felt that such direct participation in the movement interfered with his scientific work, once saying bitterly that the International hung upon him "like an incubus," and he refused to take part in several congresses in order to continue writing *Capital*, whose completion he regarded as extremely important for the movement as well as from other points of view.

Yet in the *Inaugural Address*, in numerous documents, statements, and lectures, and finally in the *Address on the Civil War in France*, he developed the concept of an international labor movement based on a scientific insight into social development, the recognition of the existence of different pre-conditions for the struggle in different countries, and international solidarity. Only in 1873, ten years before his death, when the International went into dissolution, did Marx retire from direct participation in organized activity.

The *Inaugural Address* set the workers the task of capturing political power, but it also emphasized the need to force the

State to recognize the workers' demands even before the social revolution. Concerning the English Ten Hours' Bill it states:

> This struggle about the legal restriction of the hours of labor raged the more fiercely since, apart from frightened avarice, it told indeed upon the great contest between the blind rule of the supply and demand laws which form the political economy of the middle class, and social production controlled by economic foresight, which forms the political economy of the working class. Hence the Ten Hours' Bill was not only a great practical success; it was the victory of a principle; it was the first time that in broad daylight the political economy of the middle class succumbed to the political economy of the working class.[178]

At the same time the *Address* evaluated the cooperative societies of its time as concrete proof of the historical outdatedness of capitalist ownership of the means of production, even if they were by no means as yet capable of breaking the capitalist monopoly:

> By deed, instead of by argument, they have shown that production on a large scale, and in accord with the behests of modern science, may be carried on without the existence of a class of masters employing a class of hands; that to bear fruit, the means of labor need not be monopolized as a means of dominion over, and of extortion against, the laboring man himself; and that, like slave labor, like serf labor, hired labor is but a transitory and inferior form, destined to disappear before associated labor plying its toil with a willing hand, a ready mind, and a joyous heart.[179]

Labor movements must also intervene in the foreign policies of their respective countries, watch the diplomatic acts of their governments, master the mysteries of international politics and vindicate the simple laws of morals and justice, such as ought to govern relations between private individuals, as "the rules paramount of the intercourse of nations." Like the *Communist Manifesto*, the *Address* ends with the words: Proletarians of all countries, Unite!

It is not without interest that the International was founded at a demonstration of solidarity with the oppressed Poles; and it was in reference to the Irish question that Marx pronounced his famous dictum that a nation cannot be free so long as it oppresses others.

Within the framework of the International's activities Marx allotted a most important place to trade unions and to sociopolitical claims. *Wages, Price, and Profit*, an address delivered to the General Council of the International, was in essence a detailed reply to the argument that higher wages must inevitably lead to higher prices. The English trade unions (whose earliest beginnings can be traced back to the period in the eighteenth century which followed the repeal of laws regulating wages and labor conditions) felt Marx's arguments to be of direct help to them. The Geneva Congress of the International in 1866—a Congress Marx did not attend because of his work on *Capital*—affirmed that labor protection laws do not strengthen the ruling power but modify the relationship of forces in the interest of the workers. The same congress also demanded the eight-hour day and described the trade unions as the means of opposing the numerical strength of the proletariat to the concentrated social power of capital.

The importance of the trade unions was also stressed in a circular letter of the International dealing with the views of Bakunin and the sections dominated by his supporters.* In this circular Marx wrote:

> The first phase of the struggle of the proletariat against the bourgeoisie is characterized by the movement of sects. This has some justice at a time when the proletariat is not yet sufficiently developed to act as a class. Isolated thinkers undertake the critique of the social contradictions and want to remove them by fanciful solutions which the mass of the workers has only to accept, propagate and put into action. It is in the nature of the sects which form around such pioneers that they alienate themselves from the trade unions and, in a word, from every mass movement. The mass of the proletariat remains indifferent or even hostile towards their propaganda. The workers of Paris and Lyons care as little for the Saint-Simonists,**

---

* *Michael Bakunin* (1814-1876): Russian socialist and anarchist, center of the Russian socialist emigration in central and western Europe, who vied with Marx for leadership of the the International from 1868 to 1873. He advocated the abolition of the state, religion, and marriage; quite generally, he rejected the notion of any power being exercised by men over other men.

** *Saint-Simonists*: followers of French social critic Claude-Henri de Rouvroy, Count Saint-Simon (1760-1825). Criticizing the economic egoism of the bourgeoisie, Saint-Simon wanted to solve the social problem by the moral renewal of mankind, attacked property, and demanded community ownership of the means of production. His theories had a great influence on French socialism in the nineteenth century.

the Fourierists,* and the Icarians,** as do the English Chartists†
and trade unionists for the Owenites.††

Originally a lever of the movement, they become an impediment to it
as soon as they are overtaken by it. Then they become reactionary.[180]

The argument with Bakunin's supporters, who insisted on
mandatory atheism, the abolition of all religious practices,
immediate abolition of the laws of inheritance, etc., and
refused any activity that did not lead directly and immediately
to the triumph of the working class, was directed above all at
the phraseology of sectarianism within the labor movement.
Marx dismissed their program as a hotch-potch of hackneyed
commonplaces and thoughtless twaddle, a string of empty-
headed notions aimed merely at a certain momentary effect.
As for the immediate abolition of the laws of inheritance, slave
ownership was not the result of laws which permitted such
ownership, but the other way about. Abolition of the laws of
inheritance was no more a starting point for social revolution

---

* *Fourierists*: followers of French social philosopher Charles Fourier
(1772-1837), who outlined a comprehensive system of utopian socialism
in the form of a federative association of small autarchic communities
aimed at peace and happiness. Fourier's doctrine of integrated
production, consumption, and living communities, influenced the
development of trade union organizations.

** *Icarians*: followers of French utopian communist Etienne Cabet
(1788-1856), whose book *Voyage to Icaria* (1842) sketched out an ideal
communist society.

† *Chartists*: the first democratic socialist workers' movement in
England, formed around 1832. Their "People's Charter" of 1838
demanded universal male suffrage, parliamentary reform, and social
legislation. Following the Charter's rejection by Paliament and the
suppression of a rebellion in Birmingham in 1839, time, Chartism was
finally superseded by the growing English trade union movement
around 1848. It had a lasting formative effect on the development of
class consciousness among the masses, especially through its creation
of the first independent workers' press.

†† *Owenites*: followers of the English social reformer and socialist,
Robert Owen (1771-1858), the first industrialist to introduce shorter
working hours, limitation of child labor, sickness benefits, old age
pensions, etc. In his later years he followed markedly utopian
tendencies. Owen may be considered the founder of the English trade
unions.

than abolition of the laws governing contracts between buyers and sellers was possible so long as commodity exchange existed. Marx's sensitivity towards sectarianism is clearly demonstrated in the following letter written to his son-in-law, Paul Lafargue, on April 18, 1870:

Dear Paul-Laurent,

I send enclosed the credentials for M. H. Vernet. Let him give to the new section he is about to establish no *sectarian* "*name*," either Communistic or other. Il faut éviter les "*ètiquettes*" sectaires dans L'Association Internationale. The general aspirations and tendencies of the working class emanate from the real conditions in which it finds itself placed. They are therefore common to the whole class although the movement reflects itself in their heads in the most diversified forms, more or less phantastical, more or less adequate. Those to interpret best the hidden sense of the class struggle going on before our eyes—the Communists—are the last to commit the blunder of affecting or fostering Sectarianism.[181]

True, Marx was equally allergic to all the vague phrases of "too-wise pundits" who wanted to give a "higher idealistic twist" to socialism, i.e. to replace the materialist basis (which requires serious objective study if one desires to operate upon it) by a modern mythology with its goddesses Liberty, Equality and Fraternity. In the *Critique of the Gotha Programme*, Marx was harsh in his dismissal of all vague and muddled formulations.

When the young Marx first met Parisian workers who professed the Communal ideal, he was immensely struck by the nobility that shone in their faces. The *Address of the General Council of the International*, which, under the title of *The Civil War in France*, describes and comments on the struggles and the end of the Paris Commune, is full of admiration for the militancy and self-sacrifice of the workers of Paris and for their deep sense of solidarity. We have already referred to some theoretical aspects of this work. On April 12, 1872 Marx wrote to his friend Kugelmann:

What elasticity, what historical initiative, what a capacity for sacrifice in these Parisians! After six months of hunger and ruin, caused rather by internal treachery than by the external enemy, they rise, beneath Prussian bayonets, as if there had never been a war between France and Germany and the enemy were not at the gates of Paris. History has no like example of a like greatness....

Compare these Parisians, storming heaven, with the slaves to heaven of the German-Prussian Holy Roman Empire, with its posthumous masquerades reeking of the barracks, the Church, cabbage-junkerdom and above all, of the philistine....[182]

The Address itself closed with the words:

Working men's Paris, with its Commune, will be for ever celebrated as the glorious harbinger of a new society. Its martyrs are enshrined in the great heart of the working class. Its exterminators history has already nailed to that eternal pillory from which all the prayers of the priests will not avail to redeem them.[183]

It was genuine modesty linked with deep respect for the great struggles and sacrifices of working people which made Marx write concerning certain events within the German social-democratic movement:

"I bear no grudge" (as Heine has it), and neither does Engels. Neither of us gives tuppence for popularity. Example of my dislike for any personality cult: during the time of the International I never allowed the numerous manoeuvres to acclaim me, by which I was plagued from various countries, to penetrate into the sphere of publicity, nor have I ever replied to them, except now and then with a slap.[184]

13
THE PHILOSOPHY OF PRACTICE

Marx's revolutionary humanism—his conception of human freedom as the development of the whole human being—was rooted in his "philosophy of praxis" (or practice). It contests both idealism, according to which the intellect, standing above society, is the principal force for change, and abstract materialism, which glorifies sensuous human activity in opposition to the world of the intellect. Social realty must be understood, as Fischer puts it, as the interaction "of objective circumstances and human activity." Genuine science in the social realm demands a historical perspective—not simply of the past, but of the present and the future. It demands that one "step outside" present-day society in order to view it in terms of the developmental process of which it is a part. Those who are interested in changing the world—the revolutionary forces of society—are thus best situated to both understand and interact with the dynamic character of society, including the direction of its development. For Marx, there was no conflict between genuine science and revolutionary practice.—*JBF*

The chief defect of all materialism up to now (including Feuerbach's) is that the object, reality, which we apprehend through our senses, is understood only in the form of the *object of contemplation*; but not as *sensuous human activity*, as *practice*; not subjectively. Hence in opposition to materialism the *active* side was developed abstractly by idealism—which of course does not know real sensuous activity as such.[185]

With these sentences begin the eleven theses on the materialist philosopher Ludwig Feuerbach which Marx entered in his notebook in 1845 but which, unfortunately, he never developed to a complete "philosophy of practice." [See appendix for the complete *Theses on Feuerbach*.] "The brilliant germ of the new world outlook," as Engels called these notes, did, of course, ripen in later economic, sociological, and political

148

writings. In this sketch of a new philosophy there beats the pulse of a life's work. And yet it is a pity that Marx never found time to combine into a major work what he had noted down and later in many respects developed.

In the limited space available to us and which perhaps we have already filled too densely, a few brief indications must suffice.

The "philosophy of practice" is intimately connected with the vision of the "whole," "total" man. From the very start the species man has not appropriated the world *passively* but *actively*, through practice, labor, the setting of goals, the giving of form. As men *changed* the world they expanded and refined their ability to *know* it, and the growing capacity for cognition again enhanced their ability to change it. Man creates himself by his works; by his estrangement from himself he becomes his own creator.

But the process of the division of labor led to a profound split between intellectual and physical work. In the commodity-producing society philosophy ceased to be the business of the *active* man and became that of the *contemplative* man, the man who does not change the world but observes it, reflects upon it, interprets it.

A curious inversion had taken place in the development of philosophy. In *idealist philosophy* the intellectual became the *active*, creative principle; for Fichte, the "I" (not the individual but the cosmic I) was the world creator; for Hegel, the "world spirit" works itself through all stages of "estrangement" to an all-embracing self-consciousness. For the *materialist philosophers*, on the other hand, man was only a *product* of the outside world and that world itself only an *object* for contemplation, reflected in sensory impressions, of which thoughts were regarded as the abstraction.

The "philosophy of practice" transfers the active, creative principle from the systems of idealist philosophy into materialism: reality as process, movement, change, and *social reality* as the *interaction* of objective and subjective factors, of *objective* circumstances and *human* activity.

Men are thinking beings; but the extent to which "objective truth is an attribute of human thought," the Second Thesis states,

> is not a theoretical but a *practical* question. Man must prove the truth, i.e. the reality and power, the "this-sidedness" of his thinking

in practice. The dispute over the reality or non-reality of thinking that is isolated from practice is a purely *scholastic* question.

Thus truth is an attribute of thought in so far as thought corresponds to reality; and only practice can prove the extent to which it does so. If a theory fails in practice, that is to say if practice contradicts it not only momentarily but persistently over a long period, the theory must either be rejected or corrected. Faced with a momentary, transient contradiction in practice it may be correct or approximately correct, but it must prove its power and reality by its development. Practice always decides.

Men are *active* beings; they change, so far as they are able, the circumstances they find to their advantage. "All social life is essentially *practical*," states the Eighth Thesis. "All the mysteries which urge theory into mysticism find their rational solution in human practice and in the comprehension of this practice." Human practice alone is not enough; in the "wood of blindness" a madman can lead men to disaster. It must be *comprehended* practice. To comprehend it is the function of revolutionary philosophy. This philosophy does not proceed from categories, not from general, broad principles, but from men; it examines *what* they do, asks *why* they do it, for what purpose and under what compulsion, it teaches them to *know* what they do, that is to say, it learns from practice so as to teach practice to become *self-cognition*.

The philosophy of practice denies both the assumption that man is *autonomous* and can decide independently at any time, and the opposite, i.e. that man only *appears* to decide, while in reality circumstances rule men's lives and do not admit of any genuine decision. "Man" is an abstraction: there are only men, human beings, who have their species-nature—the nature that distinguishes them from all other organisms—in common, but who belong to a particular social formation, a class, a nation, a historical epoch and are therefore *conditioned* by the totality of these circumstances in their mode of behavior, their possibilities, needs and decisions at any given time.

"The essence of man," Marx retorts to Feuerbach, "is no abstraction inherent in each separate individual. In its reality it is the *ensemble* (aggregate) of social relations." Feuerbach postulates "an abstract—*isolated*—human individual" and therefore does not see "that the abstract individual whom he analyzes belongs to a particular form of society." (Sixth and Seventh Theses.) The *concrete* human being is therefore to be understood not only as "'genus,' the inward, dumb generality which *naturally* unites the many individuals," but also as a *social* being creating itself and realizing its potential in its historical development. The "aggregate" of social relations which makes up the human being includes not only the momentary social condition but also *that which has become*— e.g. language, custom, tradition—and *that which is in process of becoming*, that which stirs as contradiction in the womb of established society and announces itself as a possibility.

Hence man is not an isolated "I" and is not capable of abolishing contradictions and re-educating others merely through acts of his consciousness, through "enlightenment" or "philosophy."

Philosophy needs practice in order to become effective. This principle is demonstrated in the Fourth Thesis using Feuerbach as an example:

> Feuerbach starts out from the fact of religious self-estrangement, of the duplication of the world into a religious and a secular one. His work consists in resolving the religious world into its secular basis. But that the secular basis raises itself above itself and establishes for itself an independent realm in the clouds can be explained only through the cleavage and self-contradictions within this secular basis. The latter must therefore in itself be both understood in its contradiction and revolutionized in practice.

Marx strongly emphasized the material and social conditioning of all human thought and action, i.e. he completely rejected "voluntarism," the notion that the human will is capable of overcoming the limitations of given circumstances. But, equally, he was convinced of the capacity of men to change these given circumstances. "The materialistic doctrine concerning the changing of circumstances and education forgets that circumstances are changed by men and that the educator himself must be educated." (Third Thesis.)

It seems to us that this *dynamism* inherent in the philosophy of practice gains special significance in an age when immense, apparently independent power apparatuses and mechanisms set in motion by the rapidly growing productive forces tend to make us feel that man is nothing and that the product is all, and somehow creates independently from human striving, knowledge, and action. The "systems," "structures," "orders" are supposed to follow immutable laws of their own, and any attempt to fight this is viewed as romantic, antiquated humanism. The anti-human is considered, as it were, a cosmic law and total surrender to total reification is a consequence of scientific thinking and deep-frozen knowledge. Ours is therefore a time when we can least of all afford to forget that men, though they are formed by circumstances, are at the same time capable of changing circumstances; the great problem always being that the educator himself must be educated, that the changing of circumstances requires changed men (or rather men engaged in changing themselves), that the humanization of society is not a natural process but presupposes human beings with unusual moral and intellectual qualities—human beings capable of transcending given circumstances.

A materialism which merely *contemplates* the world and regards it as the *object* of scientific observation does not go beyond the limits of the given situation, i.e. of bourgeois society. Refusing to criticize or to set itself any aim, it becomes willy-nilly an *affirmation of what exists*. "The highest point to which contemplative materialism can attain, i.e. that materialism which does not comprehend our sensuous nature as practical activity, is the contemplation of separate individuals and of civil society." (Ninth Thesis.) When this materialism no longer contemplates the separate individuals but regards them only as statistical units, as representatives of average modes of behavior, it becomes the philosophy, freed of all humanism, of bourgeois society at a late stage of development. For individual man is more than an invention of individualism.

"The standpoint of the old type of materialism is civil society, the standpoint of the new materialism is human society or social humanity." (Tenth Thesis.)

The *Theses on Feuerbach* were the foundation for this new materialism beginning and ending with man, a humanist philosophy of practice. If the standpoint of this philosophy is human society or social humanity, it adopts the standpoint of an as yet unattained level of development, a real but as yet unrealized possibility. In it, social tendencies concentrate into aims. In it, the self-cognition of practice becomes one of the essential factors of practice.

Philosophy without practice dissolves very easily into air or smoke or congeals into a dogmatic profession of faith: practice without philosophy turns into myopic, mindless practicism.

The philosophy of practice is a philosophy, i.e. not merely a collection of partial scientific findings from various spheres of study, but an attempt to understand the workings of a *total process*. It is the philosophy of *practice*, i.e. not merely thought drawn from and tested against practice, but also thought that helps practice towards self-cognition and thus contributes to its development.

By observing and interpreting changes as they occur, the philosophy of practice gains cognition which is never at a standstill; by the never-ending endeavor to affect the development of the changing world, it continually transcends pure observation and interpretation and becomes a motive force of practice. The celebrated Eleventh Thesis with which the notes on Feuerbach end is, therefore, not an either/or but a synthesis of philosophical interpretation and of the practical transforming of the world:

"The philosophers have only *interpreted* the world differently, the point is, to *change* it."

14
MARXISM TODAY

Marxism begins with Marx, it does not end with him. For years, Marxism was viewed as a fixed formula in which capitalist modernization would give birth to, and be rapidly superceded by, a new socialist civilization in the most industrially developed countries, that would then spread to the hinterlands. The best Marxist theory after Marx, however, followed his example in trying to analyze, as a historical process, the changing nature of capitalism and prospects for social revolution. V.I. Lenin applied this method in his theorizing that in the twentieth century, with the development of monopoly capitalism or imperialism, "the whole world was drawn into the capitalist system," creating scenarios for the class struggle that did not exist in Marx's day.★

Fischer, describing the important breakthroughs in late-1960s Marxist thought, refers to the "application of dialectical materialism to history," which he traces back to Engels. (Marx never used the term "dialectical materialism" or advocated any closed system of thought, contrary to most latter-day critics—and defenders—of Marxism.) Theoreticians in the mainstream of the Second (Socialist) and Third (Communist) International, and other political tendencies, using their own interpretations of dialectics, taught that history could be explained as the result of fixed laws in the physical universe. At the time this book was written, Fischer noted important moves toward a more flexible approach to dialectics, away from the rigid, ahistorical formulae associated with the self-justifying theories of the Stalin era. These moves did indeed help bring new approaches to Marxism—in some cases, re-energizing theory and practice; in others, producing a safe, nonrevolutionary hodgepodge.

After World War II, as Fischer notes, intellectuals like Erich Fromm and Jean-Paul Sartre responded to the emptiness of modern society with a renewed emphasis on the humanist philosophical aspects of Marxism. This variant brought Marx's insights into alienation to the

---

★ See Lenin, *Imperialism, The Highest Stage of Capitalism* (1916).

study of human psychology and sociology, influencing such germinal thinkers as Simone de Beauvoir, Herbert Marcuse, and Frantz Fanon. In contrast, structural Marxists like Louis Althusser and Nicos Poulantzas downplayed humanism by applying a structuralist interpretation of knowledge to Marxism, reframing its ideas and discoveries as a set of abstract concepts within an "overdetermining" structure (see Introduction).

Fischer's fourth variant of Marxism, focusing on "the study of history and of political initiative," is the one he found most in accord with Marx's own thinking. This perspective views history as a process in which human beings "make" their own society, though not entirely under conditions of their own choosing. It recognizes that the openness of history demands a dynamic and developing approach to the philosophy of praxis. This tradition extends from Marx to the great diversity of revolutionary thinkers and protagonists around the world, far beyond the confines of movements marching under the various banners of Marxism.

With the demise of the Soviet Union and the transformation of the superstructure of world society, the importance of Marx's vision has only broadened. The principal object of Marx's critique was always capitalism, and as long as capitalism survives, his ideas will resonate among the "wretched of the earth."—*JBF*

The world of Marx's ideas is not a closed system. Development, amplification, enlargement are intrinsic in it. To treat it in Marx's own spirit is to speak of its history, its past, its present, and of its future, which has already begun.

After Marx's death, around the turn of the century, his ideas permeated the labor movements, especially in Germany, Austria, and Russia, and helped to form the worldview of hundreds of thousands of people, acquiring, however, the accent of natural history which turned the desired development towards a socialist society into an "iron Must of history" and, even after heavy defeats, kept alive the conviction that "the world is ours despite everything." Not the least cause of this was the fact that Karl Kautsky, the principal popularizer of Marxism, had a background of Darwinism and, invoking certain passages of Marx, but more especially Engels, imposed on the Marxist view of history a determinism deriving from natural history. The most important critique of this view of history was undoubtedly Lenin's *What Is To Be Done?* (1902).

Proceeding from Marx's reflections, Lenin adapted the theory of revolution to the particular problems of Tsarist Russia. Unused reserves for bourgeois revolution could, Lenin thought, become the fuel for a socialist one, though only—in view of the already advanced level of economic development—under the leadership of the proletariat. The latter had first of all to win over the peasant masses in order to carry through the unsolved tasks of the bourgeois agrarian revolution: then the development would be driven forward to socialist revolution under the leadership of the proletariat. It is true that, even shortly before the October Revolution, Lenin still believed that the revolutionary development in Russia would only play the role of an initial detonator of the socialist revolution which—in accordance with Marx's idea—had to take place in the advanced capitalist countries.

Proceeding from Marx, invoking Marx, Lenin coupled this idea with an analysis of structural changes within capitalism. The latter, he said, had developed from a capitalism of free competition to monopoly capitalism, as Hilferding in particular had shown.★

Lenin termed this stage of capitalism—monopoly capitalism—*imperialism*. It meant that the whole world was drawn into the capitalist system; hence the revolutionary perspectives were concentrated on world revolution, which did not necessarily have to begin in an industrially developed country and by no means had to occur simultaneously in the most advanced capitalist countries. Lenin attached decisive importance to the national revolutionary movements in the colonies and semicolonies.

Leninism was the term applied during Lenin's lifetime to the ideas of that group (the Bolsheviks) of which Lenin had been the leader within Russian social democracy and under whose leadership the October Revolution of 1917 took place. After Lenin's death these views were simplified into a system which Stalin named Marxism-Leninism, or "Marxism in the era of imperialism and proletarian revolution." Mao Zedong

---

★ *Rudolf Hilferding* (1877-1941): German financial expert and social democrat, twice German finance minister in periods of crisis.

invoked this system when developing a theory of revolution which linked the problems of agrarian revolution with the national and anticolonial revolution and which viewed the peasants as the principal force in the revolutionary struggle, although with formal recognition of the leadership of the proletariat.

At the present time we can distinguish four principal variants of Marxist thought which are of effective interest for the future:

(a) Marxism as the world view of scientific thinkers who regard the Marxist theory of history as an application of dialectical materialism to history. This view is founded on the works of Engels rather than of Marx, but has, of late, also taken account of Engels's dictum that materialism must change with every important new discovery. With this in mind, Engels's own ideas are being reconsidered, his simplifications are being eliminated, and certain prohibitions, which proclaimed important discoveries of modern science to be un-Marxist, are being removed.

(b) Marxism as the "philosophy of man," with alienation as the fundamental concept.

(c) Marxism as a hierarchically organized structure of concepts distinguished by the novelty of its sphere of problems and its conceptual network. This is an attempt to apply structuralism, which has opened up valuable new ground in linguistics and in the analysis of myths, to Marxist theory and, by the "symptomatic" reading of Marx, to discover those nodal points in the structure of concepts of which Marx himself was not conscious.

(d) The interpretation of Marxism as a scientific methodology of the study of history and of political initiative. This variant corresponds to the ideas which we developed in the chapters on *Historical Materialism* and *The Philosophy of Practice*. It was represented especially by Antonio Gramsci, who represented an unorthodox trend in the socialist movement before World War I and in the communist movement between the wars.★

★ *Antonio Gramsci* (1891-1937): intellectual leader of Italian communism, author of important works of philosophy, sociology, history, and literary criticism, written for the most part in jail.

On this basis religious believers, too, are able to profess Marxism.

The influence of Marx today transcends the boundaries of Marxism; We find that the modern social sciences—sociology, political economy, historical theory, etc.—have absorbed many of the important ideas developed by Marx, so that, as C. Wright Mills wrote, these sciences are unimaginable without them ... if only as something to contest.*

---

* *C. Wright Mills* (1916-1962): leading U.S. sociologist, author of *White Collar*, *The Power Elite*, etc.

APPENDIX

Paul M. Sweezy: *Marx's Method*

From *The Theory of Capitalist Development* (1942).

Discussions of methodology in economics, as in other fields, are likely to be tiresome and unrewarding. Nevertheless, to avoid the problem altogether is to risk serious misunderstanding. In this chapter, therefore, we shall attempt as briefly as possible to set forth the chief elements in Marx's approach to economics. This is the more important in Marx's case since many of his original and significant contributions are precisely of a methodological character. Lukács, one of the most penetrating of contemporary Marxists, has even gone so far as to assert that "orthodoxy in questions of Marxism relates exclusively to method."[1]

1. THE USE OF ABSTRACTION

From a formal point of view Marx's economic methodology may appear strikingly similar to that of his classical predecessors and his neoclassical successors. He was a strong adherent of the abstract-deductive method which was such a marked characteristic of the Ricardian school. "In the analysis of economic forms," he wrote in the Preface to *Capital*, "neither microscopes nor chemical reagents are of use. The force of abstraction must replace both." Moreover, Marx believed in and practiced what modern theorists have called the method of "successive approximations," which consists in moving from the more abstract to the more concrete in a step-by-step fashion, removing simplifying assumptions at successive stages of the investigation so that theory may take account of and explain an ever wider range of actual phenomena.

When we inquire farther, however, we find striking differences between Marx and the representatives of the classical and neoclassical tradition. The principle of abstraction is itself powerless to yield knowledge; the difficult questions concern the manner

of its application. In other words, one must somehow decide what
to abstract from and what not to abstract from. Here at least two
issues arise. First, what problem is being investigated? And,
second, what are the essential elements of the problem? If we
have the answer to these questions, we shall surely know what
we cannot abstract from, and, within these limits, we shall be
able to frame our assumptions according to criteria of conve-
nience and simplicity. Now, we need go no further than the first
question to convince ourselves that economists have not always
been in agreement on their objectives. The problems which
several well-known economists have set themselves for investigation may be cited: "the nature and causes of the wealth of
nations" (Adam Smith); "the laws which regulate the distribution
of the produce of the earth" (Ricardo); "man's actions in the
ordinary business of life" (Marshall); "price and its causes and
its corollaries" (Davenport); "human behavior as a relationship
between ends and scarce means which have alternative uses"
(Robbins). No doubt there is overlapping here, but it is doubtful
if any two could be regarded as identical. From this it follows that
no two investigators will handle their materials—including the
manner in which they apply the weapon of abstraction—in
exactly the same way. One may abstract from a difference which
another is trying to explain, yet each may be justified from the
point of view of the problem which he is studying. This must be
particularly kept in mind by the student of Marx, since his
objective—"to lay bare the economic law of motion of modern
society"[2]—is radically different from that of non-Marxian schools
of thought.

Even after the investigator's task has been determined, however, there is still no sovereign formula to guide his footsteps. As
Hegel very correctly remarked in the Introduction to his *Philosophy of History*: in the "process of scientific understanding, it is
of importance that the essential should be distinguished and
brought into relief in contrast with the so-called non-essential.
But in order to render this possible we must know what *is
essential*...." To bring the essential into relief and to make
possible its analysis: that is the specific task of abstraction. But
where to start? How to distinguish the essential from the non-
essential? Methodology can pose these questions, but unfortunately it cannot provide ready-made answers. If it could, the
"process of scientific understanding" would be a far more routine
matter than it actually is. In practice, it is necessary to formulate
hypotheses about what is essential, to work these hypotheses
through, and to check the conclusions against the data of

experience. If we are to understand the achievement of a particular scientist we must, therefore, try to identify his key hypotheses and to see, if possible, where he gets them from and how he
develops their implications. It need hardly be pointed out that
this is not always an easy matter, but in the case of Marx we
know enough about his intellectual development to make the
attempt.

As a student at the university, Marx concentrated in jurisprudence and philosophy and planned to enter upon an academic
career. His "radical" leanings—though at the time he was not even
a socialist—prevented his getting a teaching position, and in
1842 he accepted the editorship of the newly founded *Rheinische
Zeitung*. In this capacity he came into contact for the first time
with actual social problems and also with new social ideas,
particularly the socialist and communist ideas which were ema-
nating from France in such quantities in the 1830s and 1840s.
In a controversy with the *Augsburger Zeitung*, Marx was somewhat discomfited to discover that he did not know what to think
of socialism; he therefore resolved at the first opportunity to give
the subject the serious study which he was convinced it merited.
The opportunity was not long in coming; in a few months the
Rheinische Zeitung was shut down by the authorities, and Marx
found himself a free agent. He immediately plunged into an
intensive study of socialism and communism, of French history,
and of English political economy. It was during the next few
years, spent mostly in Paris and Brussels, that he broke with his
philosophic past and achieved the mature point of view from
which he was to write later economic works. In short, his
approach to economics was shaped and determined long before
he decided to make the study of economics his primary concern.

We have in the justly famous Preface to *The Critique of Political
Economy* a statement by Marx concerning his intellectual development during these crucial years. Though many readers will be
familiar with this preface, it may perhaps not be amiss to
reproduce a portion of it here. (The italics are added.)*

> I was led by my studies [he wrote] to the conclusion that legal
> relations as well as forms of state could neither be understood by
> themselves, nor explained by the so-called general progress of the

---

* *Editor's note*: The translation cited here is different from the extract
from the Preface to *A Contribution to the Critique of Political Economy*
that appears in this appendix beginning on p. 171.

human mind, but that they are rooted in the material conditions of life which are summed up by Hegel after the fashion of the English and French of the eighteenth century under the name "civil society"; *the anatomy of that civil society is to be sought in political economy.* The study of the latter which I had taken up in Paris, I continued at Brussels.... The general conclusion at which I arrived and which, *once reached, continued to serve as the leading thread in my studies,* may be briefly summed up as follows: In the social production which men carry on they enter into definite relations that are independent of their will; these relations of production correspond to a definite stage of development of their material powers of production. The sum total of these relations of production constitutes the economic structure of society—the real foundation on which rise legal and political superstructures and to which correspond definite forms of social consciousness. The mode of production in material life determines the general character of the social, political, and spiritual processes of life. It is not the consciousness of men that determines their existence, but, on the contrary, their social existence determines their consciousness. At a certain stage of their development, the material forces of production in society come in conflict with the existing relations of production, or—what is but a legal expression for the same thing—with the property relations within which they had been at work before. From forms of development of the forces of production these relations turn into their fetters. Then comes the period of social revolution. With the change of the economic founda-tion the entire immense superstructure is more or less rapidly transformed.

It is apparent from this that Marx's primary interest was society as a whole, and, more especially, the process of social change. Political Economy—the "anatomy" of society—is signifi-cant not primarily for its own sake but because it is in this sphere that the impetus to social change is to be found. It must be emphasized, because the contrary has so often been asserted, that Marx was not trying to reduce everything to economic terms. He was rather attempting to uncover the true interrelation between the economic and the non-economic factors in the totality of social existence.

Once having reached the conclusion that the key to social change is to be found in movements of the mode of production, Marx was in effect committed to an exhaustive study of political economy from the standpoint of the laws governing changes in the mode of production. "To lay bare the economic law of motion of modern society" now became the scientific goal to which he devoted most of the remainder of his life.

How, given this objective, could one recognize the essential aspects of the problem? Marx retained, because they seemed to stand up under searching studies into the actuality of historical development, those elements of Hegel's thought which emphasized process and development through the conflict of opposed or contradictory forces. Unlike Hegel, however, he traced decisive historical conflicts to roots in the mode of production; that is, he discovered them to be what he called class conflicts. Thus the *Communist Manifesto* (1847), after an introductory note, begins: "The history of all hitherto existing society is the history of class struggles." The economic forces at work manifest themselves in class conflicts under capitalism as under earlier forms of society. It follows that the essential economic relations are those which underlie and express themselves in the form of class conflict. These are the essential elements which must be isolated and analyzed through the method of abstraction.

Even this hypothesis, however, could lead to divergent procedures. The classical economists were also very much interested in the economic roots of class conflicts—in a sense this is exactly what "the distribution of the produce of the earth" meant to Ricardo—but the social antagonism which occupied most of their attention, both intellectual and emotional, was the conflict between industrial capitalists and landlords. Consequently they placed great, sometimes predominant, emphasis on land and the income derived from the ownership of land. Indeed, without a knowledge of "the true doctrine of rent," Ricardo asserted, "it is impossible to understand the effect of the progress of wealth on profits and wages, or to trace satisfactorily the influence of taxation on different classes of the community...."[3] Marx recognized the tendency to lay primary emphasis on land and rent, but he regarded it as misguided. "Nothing seems more natural," he wrote, "than to start with rent, with landed property, since it is bound up with land, the source of all production and all existence, and with the first form of production in all more or less settled communities, viz., agriculture."[4] Nevertheless, he added at once, "nothing could be more erroneous." His reason for adopting this attitude is the key to his subsequent procedure.

In capitalist society,

> agriculture comes to be more and more merely a branch of industry and is completely dominated by capital.... *Capital is the all-dominating power of bourgeois society.* It must form the starting point as well as the end and be developed before land ownership is....

> It would thus be impractical and wrong to arrange the economic categories in the order in which they were the determining factors in the course of history. Their order of sequence is rather determined by the relation which they bear to each other in modern bourgeois

society, and which is the exact opposite of what seems to be their natural order or the order of their historical development. What we are interested in is not the place which economic relations occupy in the historical succession of different forms of society.... We are interested in their organic connection within modern bourgeois society.[5]

The italicized sentence is particularly important. That "capital is the all-dominating economic power of bourgeois society" meant to Marx, as it would have meant to one of the classical economists, that the primary economic relation is that between capitalists and workers. As he expressed the point in another place, "The relation between wage labor and capital determines the entire character of the mode of production."[6] Even before he began his researches for the *Critique* and for *Capital*, he had expressed the same judgment in the *Manifesto*: "Society as a whole is more and more splitting up into two great hostile camps, into two great classes facing each other—bourgeoisie and proletariat." This relation must form the center of investigation; the power of abstraction must be employed to isolate it, to reduce it to its purest form, to enable it to be subjected to the most painstaking analysis, free of all unrelated disturbances.

The adoption of this position requires a procedure involving at least two fairly distinct steps.

First, all social relations except that between capital and labor must be provisionally assumed away, to be reintroduced, one at a time, only at a later stage of the analysis.

Second, the capital-labor relation itself must be reduced to its most significant form or forms. This is not a quantitative question; it does not mean that the most frequent, or modal, forms of the relation must be selected for analysis. Significance, in this context, is a question of the structural characteristics and tendencies of the whole society. Marx, as is well known, selected the forms of capital-labor relation which arise in the sphere of industrial production as the most significant for modern capitalist society. Capitalists and workers are alike reduced to certain standard types, from which all characteristics irrelevant to the relation under examination are removed. "Individuals are dealt with," he wrote in the Preface to *Capital*, "only in so far as they are the personifications of economic categories, embodiments of particular class relations and class interests."

What is the nature of this capital-labor relation? In form it is an exchange relation. The capitalist buys labor power from the worker; the worker receives money from the capitalist with which he acquires the necessaries of life. As an exchange relation, it is clearly a special case of a large class of such relations which have a common form and structure. It is evident, therefore, that the study of the capital-labor relation must begin with an analysis of the general phenomenon of exchange.

In this way we arrive at the actual starting point of Marx's Political Economy. Part I of the first volume of *Capital*, which summarizes the earlier *Critique of Political Economy*, is entitled "Commodities." Whatever is customarily intended for exchange rather than for direct use is a commodity; the analysis of commodities, therefore, involves the analysis of the exchange relation and its quantitative aspect (exchange value); it includes, moreover, an analysis of money. As we shall see later on, some of Marx's most interesting results arise out of the treatment of commodities.

Having laid the necessary foundation with the analysis of commodities, Marx proceeds to his main task. *Almost the entire remainder of the first volume of Capital is devoted to the capital-labor relation in its "isolated" and "purified" forms.* In other words, Volume I begins and remains on a high level of abstraction.

It is difficult for those unacquainted with Marx's method to believe that this statement can be meant seriously. They point to the wealth of factual and historical material which is such an outstanding feature of Volume I. Does this not mean that Marx was, in fact, just the reverse of abstract? This reasoning misses the point. The legitimate purpose of abstraction in social science is never to get away from the real world but rather to isolate certain aspects of the real world for intensive investigation. When, therefore, we say that we are operating on a high level of abstraction we mean that we are dealing with a relatively small number of aspects of reality; we emphatically do not mean that those aspects with which we are dealing are not capable of historical investigation and factual illustration. A cursory check-up is sufficient to indicate that the great bulk of the factual material introduced by Marx in Volume I relates directly to the capital-labor relation and is of an illustrative or historical character. It constitutes, therefore, a confirmation rather than a contradiction of the statement that Volume I begins and remains on a high level of abstraction.

The establishment of this fact allows us to draw an important corollary, namely, that the results achieved in Volume I have a provisional character. In many cases, though not necessarily in all, they undergo a more or less extensive modification on a lower level of abstraction, that is to say, when more aspects of reality are taken into account.* It follows that the tendencies or laws enunciated in Volume I are not to be interpreted as direct predictions about the future. Their validity is relative to the level of abstraction on which they are derived and to the extent of the modifications which they must undergo when the analysis is brought to a more concrete level. Recognition of this fact would have saved a great deal of sterile controversy. As an example we may cite the famous "law of the increasing misery of the proletariat," which Marx called "the absolute general law of capitalist accumulation."[7] Anti-Marxists have always maintained the falsity of this law and have deduced from this the incorrectness of Marx's analysis of capitalism.** Some Marxists, on the other hand, have been equally concerned to demonstrate the truth of the law, and so a controversy producing much heat and little light has raged for more than a half century. Both sides are guilty of the same misunderstanding of Marx's method. The law in question is derived on a high level of abstraction; the term "absolute" used in describing it is used in the Hegelian sense of "abstract"; it constitutes in no sense a concrete prediction about the future. Moreover, in this particular case, Marx says as much in perfectly clear language, so that misinterpretation seems peculiarly difficult to condone. Having stated the law, he immediately adds, "Like all other laws it is modified in its working by many circumstances, the analysis of which does not concern us here." It would be impossible to have a plainer warning not to interpret the law as a concrete prediction. A proper regard to problems of method would have rendered this misunderstanding, along with many others, unnecessary.

We need not discuss the whole plan of *Capital*. For present purposes, it is only necessary to point out that the intent of Volumes II and III was to take into account factors which were consciously left out of Volume I, that is to say, to bring the analysis to progressively lower levels of abstraction. At the same time, and in a sense paradoxically, Volumes II and III contain relatively less factual material than Volume I. This is accounted

---

* This aspect of Marx's method is well treated by Henryk Grossmann in the Introduction to his book *Das Akkumulations- und Zusammenbruchsgesetz de kapitalistischen Systems* (Leipzig, 1929).

** Grossmann cites a large number of examples in *Das Akkumulations- und Zusammenbruchsgesetz*, pp. 23 ff.

for by their unfinished state. In compiling Volumes II and III from Marx's manuscripts, Engels found a great deal of illustrative material, but it was "barely arranged, much less worked out."[8] Volume I, on the other hand, Marx prepared for the press himself, so that he was able to integrate his factual and theoretical materials in a way which Engels could not possibly have accomplished for the later volumes without going far beyond the functions of an editor, a course which he wisely declined to pursue.

We have discussed Marx's use of abstraction in general terms and do not propose at this stage to enter into particular cases. It is well to note, however, that a great many criticisms of Marx's economics are, consciously or unconsciously, based upon a rejection of the assumptions with which he works. Our discussion should help to establish criteria by which to judge the validity of these criticisms. In each case, the following three questions should be asked about the simplifying assumptions (or abstractions) which give rise to criticism: (1) are they framed with a proper regard for the problem under investigation? (2) do they eliminate the non-essential elements of the problem? (3) do they stop short of eliminating the essential elements? If all three of these questions can be answered in the affirmative, we may say that the principle of appropriate abstraction has been observed. This principle is of great assistance in testing the relevance and validity of a considerable range of Marx criticism.

2. THE HISTORICAL CHARACTER OF MARX'S THOUGHT

Marx's method, says Lukács, "is in its innermost essence historical."[9] This is certainly correct, and no discussion of the problem which fails to emphasize it can be regarded as satisfactory.*

For Marx, social reality is not so much a specified set of relations, still less a conglomeration of things. It is rather the process of change inherent in a specified set of relations. In other words, social reality is the historical process, a process which, in principle, knows no finality and no stopping places.** Social

---

* One of the best discussions in English of this aspect of Marx's thought, and, indeed, of all the problems treated in this chapter, will be found in Karl Korsch, *Karl Marx* (London: Chapman & Hall, 1938).

** "There is a continual movement of growth in productive forces, of destruction in social relations, of formation in ideas; the only immutable thing is the abstraction of movement—*mors immortalis* ['immortal death']." Marx, *The Poverty of Philosophy*.

systems, like individuals, go through a life cycle and pass from the scene when "from forms of development of the forces of production" they "turn into their fetters." The process of social change, however, is not purely mechanical; it is rather the product of human action, but action which is definitely limited by the kind of society in which it has its roots. "Men make their own history," Marx wrote, "but they do not make it just as they please; they do not make it under circumstances chosen by themselves, but under circumstances directly found, given, and transmitted from the past."[10] Society both is changing and, within limits, can be changed.

Consistent adherence to this position leads to a consistently historical approach to social science. Moreover—and this is but another aspect of the same thing—it leads to a critical approach to every form of society, including the present. The importance of this point is difficult to overstress. It is a characteristic feature of non-Marxian thought that it can comprehend the transitory character of all earlier social orders, while this same critical faculty fails when it is a question of the capitalist system itself. [...] For the typical modern thinker, as Marx expressed it, "there has been history, but there is no longer any."[11] Lukács's remark in this connection is striking:

> This un- and anti-historical core of bourgeois thought appears in its most glaring form when we consider the *problem of the present as a historical problem....* The complete incapacity of all bourgeois thinkers and historians to comprehend world-historical events of the present as world history must remain an unpleasant memory to all level-headed people since the world war and the world revolution.[12]

Nothing that has happened since 1922 could lead one to alter this judgment; rather the contrary. Marxists, on the other hand, consistently interpret contemporary events in a world-historical context. The difference is obviously not a question of intelligence; it is a question of method and approach.

Most people take capitalism for granted, just as they take the solar system for granted. The eventual passing of capitalism, which is often conceded nowadays, is thought of in much the same way as the eventual cooling of the sun, that is to say, its relevance to contemporary events is denied. From this point of view one can understand and criticize what happens within the framework of the system; one can neither understand nor evaluate what happens to the system itself. The latter fact not infrequently takes the form of a simple denial that one can meaningfully talk about social systems. Great historical events, however, generally concern whole social systems. The result is that to the typical modern mind they assume a catastrophic character, with all that this implies in the way of emotional shock and intellectual confusion.

To the Marxist, on the other hand, the specific historical (i.e., transitory) character of capitalism is a major premise. It is by virtue of this fact that the Marxist is able, so to speak, to stand outside the system and criticize it as a whole. Moreover, since human action is itself responsible for the changes which the system is undergoing and will undergo, a critical attitude is not only intellectually possible, it is also morally significant—as, for example, a critical attitude toward the solar system, whatever its shortcomings, would not be—and, last but not least, practically important.

Marx's Starting Point

Theses on Feuerbach (1845): Marx's first elaboration of his philosophical work.

I

The chief defect of all hitherto existing materialism—that of Feuerbach included—is that the thing [*Gegenstand*], reality, sensuousness, is conceived only in the form of the *object* [*Objekt*] or of *contemplation* [*Anschauung*], but not as *sensuous human activity, practice* [*Praxis*], not subjectively. Hence it happened that the *active* side, in contradistinction to materialism, was developed by idealism—but only abstractly, since, of course, idealism does not know real, sensuous activity as such. Feuerbach wants sensuous objects, really differentiated from the thought objects, but he does not conceive human activity itself as *objective* [*gegenständliche*] activity. Hence, in *The Essence of Christianity*, he regards the theoretical attitude as the only genuinely human attitude, while practice is conceived and fixed only in its dirty-judaical formof appearance. Hence he does not grasp the significance of "revolutionary," of "practical-critical" activity.

II

The question whether objective truth can be attributed to human thinking is not a question of theory but is a *practical* question. In practice man must prove the truth, that is, the reality and power, the this-sidedness [*Diesseitigkeit*] of his thinking. The dispute over the reality or non-reality of thinking which is isolated from practice is a purely *scholastic* question.

III

The materialist doctrine that men are products of circumstances and upbringing, and that, therefore, changed men are products of other circumstances and changed upbringing, forgets that it is men that change circumstances and that the educator himself needs educating. Hence, this doctrine necessarily arrives at dividing society into two parts, of which one is superior to society (in Robert Owen, for example).

The coincidence of the changing of circumstances and of human activity can be conceived and rationally understood only as *revolutionizing practice*.

IV

Feuerbach starts out from the fact of religious self-alienation, the duplication of the world into a religious, imaginary world and a real one. His work consists in the dissolution of the religious world into its secular basis. He overlooks the fact that after completing this work, the chief thing still remains to be done. For the fact that the secular foundation detaches itself from itself and establishes itself in the clouds as an independent realm is really only to be explained by the self-contradictoriness of this secular basis. The latter must itself, therefore, first be understood in its contradiction and then, by the removal of the contradiction, revolutionized in practice. Thus, for instance, once the earthly family is discovered to be the secret of the holy family, the former must then itself be criticized in theory and revolutionized in practice.

V

Feuerbach, not satisfied with *abstract thinking*, appeals to *sensuous contemplation*; but he does not conceive sensuousness as *practical*, human-sensuous activity.

VI

Feuerbach resolves the religious essence into the *human* essence. But the human essence is no abstraction inherent in each single individual. In its reality it is the ensemble of the social relations.

Feuerbach, who does not enter upon a criticism of this real essence, is consequently compelled:

1. To abstract from the historical process and to fix the religious sentiment [*Gemüt*] as something by itself, and to presuppose an abstract—*isolated*—human individual.

2. The human essence, therefore, can with him be comprehended only as a "genus," as an internal, dumb generality which merely *naturally* unites the many individuals.

VII

Feuerbach, consequently, does not see that the "religious sentiment" is itself a *social product*, and that the abstract individual whom he analyzes belongs in reality to a particular form of society.

VIII

Social life is essentially *practical.* All mysteries which mislead theory to mysticism find their rational solution in human practice and in the comprehension of this practice.

IX

The highest point attained by *comtemplative* materialism, that is, materialism which does not understand sensuousness as practical activity, is the contemplation of single individuals in "civil society."

X

The standpoint of the old materialism is "*civil*" society; the standpoint of the new is *human* society, or socialized humanity.

XI

The philosophers have only *interpreted* the world, in various ways; the point, however, is to *change* it.

The Base-Superstructure Metaphor

From the Preface to *A Contribution to the Critique of Political Economy* (1859).

... I was taking up law, which discipline, however, I only pursued as a subordinate subject along with philosophy and history. In the year 1842-1843, as editor of the *Rheinische Zeitung*, I experienced for the first time the embarrassment of having to take part in discussions on so-called material interests. The proceedings of the Rhenish Landtag on thefts of wood and parcelling of landed property, the official polemic which Herr von Schaper, then *Oberprasident* of the Rhine Province, opened against the *Rheinische Zeitung* on the conditions of the Moselle peasantry, and finally debates on free trade and protective tariffs provided the first occasions for occupying myself with economic questions. On the other hand, at that time when the good will to "go farther" greatly outweighed knowledge of the subject, a philosophically weakly tinged echo of French Socialism and Communism made itself audible in the *Rheinische Zeitung*. I declared myself against this amateurism, but frankly confessed at the same time in a controversy with the *Allgemeine Augsburger Zeitung* that my previous studies did not permit me even to venture any judgment on the content of the French tendencies. Instead, I eagerly seized on the illusion of the managers of the *Rheinische Zeitung*, who thought that by a weaker attitude on the part of the paper they could secure a remission of the death sentence passed upon it, to withdraw from the public stage into the study.

The first work which I undertook for a solution of the doubts which assailed me was a critical review of the Hegelian philosophy of right,* a work the introduction to which appeared in 1844 in the *Deutsch-Französische Jahrbucher*, published in Paris. My investigation led to the result that legal relations as well as forms of state are to be grasped neither from themselves nor from the so-called general development of the human mind, but rather have their roots in the material conditions of life, the sum total of which Hegel, following the example of the Englishmen and Frenchmen of the eighteenth century, combines under the name of "civil society," that however the anatomy of civil society is to be sought in political economy. The investigation of the latter, which I began in Paris, I continued in Brussels, whither I had emigrated in consequence of an expulsion order of M. Guizot. The general result at which I arrived and which, once won, served as a guiding thread for my studies, can be briefly formulated as follows: In the social production of their life, men enter into definite relations that are indispensable and independent of their will, relations of production which correspond to a definite stage of development of their material productive forces. The sum total of these relations of production constitutes the economic structure of society, the real foundation, on which rises a legal and political superstructure and to which correspond definite forms of social consciousness. The mode of production of material life conditions the social, political, and intellectual life process in general. It is not the consciousness of men that determines their being, but, on the contrary, their social being that determines their consciousness. At a certain stage of their development, the material productive forces of society come in conflict with the existing relations of production, or—what is but a legal expression for the same thing—with the property relations within which they have been at work hitherto. From forms of development of the productive forces these relations turn into their fetters. Then begins an epoch of social revolution. With the change of the

---

* *Contribution to the Critique of Hegel's Philosophy of Right* (1844).

economic foundation the entire immense superstructure is more or less rapidly transformed. In considering such transformations a distinction should always be made between the material transformation of the economic conditions of production, which can be determined with the precision of natural science, and the legal, political, religious, aesthetic, or philosophic—in short, ideological forms in which men become conscious of this conflict and fight it out. Just as our opinion of an individual is not based on what he thinks of himself, so can we not judge of such a period of transformation by its own consciousness; on the contrary, this consciousness must be explained rather from the contradictions of material life, from the existing conflict between the social productive forces and the relations of production. No social order ever perishes before all the productive forces for which there is room in it have developed; and new, higher relations of production never appear before the material conditions of their existence have matured in the womb of the old society itself. Therefore mankind always sets itself only such tasks as it can solve; since, looking at the matter more closely, it will always be found that the task itself arises only when the material conditions for its solution already exist or are at least in the process of formation. In broad outline Asiatic, ancient, feudal, and modern bourgeois modes of production can be designated as progressive epochs in the economic formation of society. The bourgeois relations of production are the last antagonistic form of the social process of production—antagonistic not in the sense of individual antagonism, but of one arising from the social conditions of life of the individuals; at the same time the productive forces developing in the womb of bourgeois society create the material conditions for the solution of that antagonism. This social formation brings, therefore, the prehistory of human society to a close.

Frederick Engels, with whom, since the appearance of his brilliant sketch on the criticism of the economic categories* (in the *Deutsch-Französische Jahrbucher*), I had maintained a constant exchange of ideas by correspondence, had by another road (compare his *The Condition of the Working Class in England* in 1844) arrived at the same result as I, and when in the spring of 1845 he also settled in Brussels, we resolved to work out in common the opposition of our view to the ideological view of German philosophy, in fact, to settle accounts with our erstwhile

---

* *Outlines of a Critique of Political Economy* (1843).

philosophical conscience. The resolve was carried out, in the form of a criticism of post-Hegelian philosophy.* The manuscript, two large octavo volumes, had long reached its place of publication in Westphalia when we received the news that altered circumstances did not allow of its being printed. We abandoned the manuscript to the gnawing criticism of the mice all the more willingly as we had achieved our main purpose—self-clarification. Of the scattered works in which we put our views before the public at that time, now from one aspect, now from another, I will mention only *The Communist Manifesto*, jointly written by Engels and myself, and *Discours sur le libre échange*,** published by me. The decisive points of our view were first scientifically, although only polemically, indicated in my work published in 1847 and directed against Proudhon: *Misere de la philosophie*,[†] etc. A dissertation written in German on *Wage Labor*, [††] in which I put together my lectures on this subject delivered in the Brussels German Workers' Society,[‡] was interrupted, while being printed, by the February Revolution[‡‡] and my consequent forcible removal from Belgium.

The editing of the *Neue Rheinische Zeitung* in 1848 and 1849, and the subsequent events, interrupted my economic studies which could only be resumed in the year 1850 in London. The enormous material for the history of political economy which is accumulated in the British Museum, the favorable vantage point afforded by London for the observation of bourgeois society, and finally new stage of development upon which the latter appeared to have entered with the discovery of gold in California and Australia, determined me to begin afresh from the very beginning and to work through the new material critically. These studies led partly of themselves into apparently quite remote subjects on which I had to dwell for a shorter of longer period. Especially, however, was the time at my disposal curtailed by the

---

* *The German Ideology* (1846).

** Speech on the question of free trade (1848).

† *The Poverty of Philosophy.*

†† *Wage Labor and Capital* (1849).

‡ A group organized to promote political education, founded by Marx and Engels in Brussels, August 1847.

‡‡ France, 1848. See Marx, *The Class Struggles in France* (1850).

imperative necessity of earning my living. My contributions, during eight years now, to the first English-American newspaper, the *New York Tribune*, compelled an extraordinary scattering of my studies, since I occupy myself with newspaper correspondence proper only in exceptional cases. However, articles on striking economic events in England and on the Continent constituted so considerable a part of my contributions that I was compelled to make myself familiar with practical details which lie outside the sphere of the actual science of political economy.

This sketch of the course of my studies in the sphere of political economy is intended only to show that my views, however they may be judged and however little they may coincide with the interested prejudices of the ruling classes, are the result of conscientious investigation lasting many years. But at the entrance to science, as at the entrance to hell, the demand must be posted:

> *Qui si convien lasciare ogni sospetto;*
> *Ogni vilta convien che qui sia morta.**

London, January 1859

The Philosophy of History

From *The Eighteenth Brumaire of Louis Bonaparte* (1852).

Hegel remarks somewhere that all facts and personages of great importance in world history occur, as it were, twice. He forgot to add: the first time as tragedy, the second as farce. Caussidière for Danton, Louis Blanc for Robespierre, the *Montagne* of 1848 to 1851 for the *Montagne* of 1793 to 1795,** the Nephew for the Uncle. And the same caricature occurs in the circumstances attending the second edition of the eighteenth Brumaire!

---

* Here all mistrust must be abandoned/And here must perish every craven thought. [Dante, The Divine Comedy]

** *The Montagne* refers to a revolutionary group from the French Revolution, whose revival was attempted in the aborted revolution of 1848.

Men make their own history, but they do not make it just as they please; they do not make it under circumstances chosen by themselves, but under circumstances directly encountered, given and transmitted from the past. The tradition of all the dead generations weights like a nightmare of the brain of the living. And just when they seem engaged in revolutionizing themselves and things, in creating something that has never yet existed, precisely in such periods of revolutionary crisis they anxiously conjure up the spirits of the past to their service and borrow from them names, battle cries, and costumes in order to present the new scene of world history in this time-honored disguise and this borrowed language. Thus Luther donned the mask of the Apostle Paul, the Revolution of 1789 to 1814 draped itself alternately as the Roman republic and the Roman empire, and the Revolution of 1848 knew nothing better to do than to parody, now 1789, now the revolutionary tradition of 1793 to 1795. In like manner, a beginner who has learned a new language always translates it back into his mother tongue, but he has assimilated the spirit of the new language and can produce freely in it only when he finds his way in it without recalling the old and forgets his native tongue in the use of the new.

Consideration of this conjuring up of the dead of world history reveals at once a salient difference. Camille Desmoulins, Danton, Robespierre, Saint-Just, Napoleon, the heroes as well as the parties and the masses of the old French Revolution, performed the task of their time in Roman costume and with Roman phrases, the task of unchaining and setting up modern bourgeois society. The first ones knocked the feudal basis to pieces and mowed off the feudal heads which had grown on it. The other created inside France the conditions under which alone free competition could be developed, parcelled landed property exploited, and the unchained industrial productive power of the nation employed; and beyond the French borders he everywhere swept the feudal institutions away, so far as was necessary to furnish bourgeois society in France with a suitable up-to-date environment on the European Continent. The new social formation once established, the antediluvian Colossi disappeared and with them disappeared Romanity— the Brutuses, Gracchi, Publicolas, the tribunes, the senators, and Caesar himself. Bourgeois society in its sober reality had begotten its true interpreters and mouthpieces in the Says, Cousins, Royer-Collards, Benjamin Constants, and Guizots; its real military leaders sat behind the office desks, and the hog-headed Louis XVIII was its political chief. Wholly absorbed in the production of wealth and in peaceful competitive struggle, it no longer comprehended that ghosts from the days of Rome had watched over its cradle. But unheroic as bourgeois society is, it nevertheless took heroism, sacrifice, terror, civil war, and battles of peoples to bring it into being. And in the classically austere traditions of the Roman republic its gladiators found the ideals and the art forms, the self-deceptions that they needed in order to conceal from themselves the bourgeois limitations of the content of their struggles and to keep their enthusiasm on the high plane of the great historical tragedy. Similarly, at another stage of development, a century earlier, Cromwell and the English people had borrowed speech, passions, and illusions from the Old Testament for their bourgeois revolution. When the real aim had been achieved, when the bourgeois transformation of English society had been accomplished, Locke supplanted Habakkuk.

Thus the awakening of the dead in those revolutions served the purpose of glorifying the new struggles, not of parodying the old; of magnifying the given task in imagination, not of fleeing from its solution in reality; of finding once more the spirit of revolution, not of making its ghost walk about again.

From 1848 to 1851 only the ghost of the old revolution walked about, from Marrast, the *républicain en gants jaunes*,* who disguised himself as the old Bailly, down to the adventurer, who hides his commonplace repulsive features under the iron death mask of Napoleon. An entire people, which had imagined that by means of a revolution it had imparted to itself an accelerated power of motion, suddenly finds itself set back into a defunct epoch and, in order that no doubt as to the relapse may be possible, the old data arise again, the old chronology, the old names, the old edicts, which had long become a subject of antiquarian erudition, and the old minions of the law, who had seemed long decayed. The nation feels like that mad Englishman in Bedlam who fancies that he lives in the times of the ancient Pharaohs and daily bemoans the hard labor that he must perform in the Ethiopian mines as a gold digger, immured in this subterranean prison, a dimly burning light fastened to his head, the overseer of the slaves behind him with a long whip, and at the exits a confused welter of barbarian mercenaries, who understand neither the forced laborers in the mines nor one

---

* Republican in yellow gloves [an anti-royalist figure with aristocratic airs].

another, since they speak no common language. "And all this is expected of me," sighs the mad Englishman, "of me, a freeborn Briton, in order to make gold for the old Pharaohs." "In order to pay the debts of the Bonaparte family," sighs the French nation. The Englishman, so long as he was in his right mind, could not get rid of the fixed idea of making gold. The French, so long as they were engaged in revolution, could not get rid of the memory of Napoleon, as the election of December 10 proved. They hankered to return from the perils of revolution to the fleshpots of Egypt, and December 2, 1851 was the answer. They have not only a caricature of the old Napoleon, they have the old Napoleon himself, caricatured as he must appear in the middle of the nineteenth century.

The social revolution of the nineteenth century cannot draw its poetry from the past, but only from the future. It cannot begin with itself before it has stripped off all superstition in regard to the past. Earlier revolutions required recollections of past world history in order to drug themselves concerning their own content. In order to arrive at its own content, the revolution of the nineteenth century must let the dead bury their dead. There the phrase went beyond the content; here the content goes beyond the phrase.

The February Revolution was a surprise attack, a *taking* of the old society *unawares*, and the people proclaimed this unhoped for *stroke* as a deed of world importance, ushering in a new epoch. On December 2 the February Revolution is conjured away by a cardsharper's trick, and what seems overthrown is no longer the monarchy but the liberal concessions that were wrung from it by centuries of struggle. Instead of *society* having conquered a new content for itself, it seems that the *state* only returned to its oldest form, to the shamelessly simple domination of the sabre and the cowl. This is the answer to the *coup de main* of February 1848, given by the *coup de tête* of December 1851.* Easy come, easy go. Meanwhile the interval of time has not passed by unused. During the years 1848 to 1851 French society has made up, and that by an abbreviated because revolutionary method, for the studies and experiences which, in a regular, so to speak textbook course of development would have had to precede the February Revolution, if it was to be more than a ruffling of the surface. Society now seems to have fallen back behind its point of

---

* *Coup de main*: surprise attack. *Coup de tête*: rash act.

departure; it has in truth first to create for itself the revolutionary point of departure, the situation, the relations, the conditions under which alone modern revolution becomes serious.

Bourgeois revolutions, like those of the eighteenth century, storm swiftly from success to success; their dramatic effects outdo each other; men and things seem set in sparkling brilliants; ecstasy is the everyday spirit; but they are short-lived; soon they have attained their zenith, and a long crapulent depression lays hold of society before it learns soberly to assimilate the results of a storm-and-stress period. On the other hand, proletarian revolutions, like those of the nineteenth century, criticize themselves constantly, interrupt themselves continually in their own course, come back to the apparently accomplished in order to begin it afresh, deride with unmerciful thoroughness the inadequacies, weaknesses, and paltrinesses of their first attempts, seem to throw down their adversary only in order that he may draw new strength from the earth and rise again, more gigantic, before them, recoil ever and anon from the indefinite prodigiousness of their own aims, until a situation has been created which makes all turning back impossible, and the conditions themselves cry out: *Hic Rhodus, hic salta!**

---

* Here is the rose, here dance! A paraphrase of Hegel's quote (Preface, *Outlines of the Philosophy of Right*) from Aesop's fable, "The Swaggerer," referring to one who boasted that he had once made a gigantic leap at Rhodes (which also means "rose" in Greek) and was challenged: "Here is Rhodes. Here leap!" In other words: Show right here by action what you can do!

NOTES

Foster: Introduction

1. Erich Fromm, *Marx's Concept of Man* (New York: Ungar, 1966), p. 1.

2. Because of the prior existence of a well-known book in English by H.B. Acton entitled *What Marx Really Said*—the literal translation of *Was Marx wirklich sagte*—English-language publishers chose alternative titles for this book, including *Marx in His Own Words* (Harmondsworth: Penguin, 1970) and *The Essential Marx* (New York: Herder and Herder, 1970). Since both English-language titles suggest that the book is a collection of excerpts from Marx, rather than an introductory guide to Marx, the title *How to Read Karl Marx* is used here instead.

3. Ernst Fischer, *The Necessity of Art* (Harmondsworth: Penguin, 1963); Franz Marek, *Philosophy of World Revolution* (New York: International Publishers, 1969).

4. Samuel H. Beer, "Introduction," in Karl Marx and Friedrich Engels, *The Communist Manifesto* (Arlington Heights, IL: Harlan Davidson, Inc., 1955), pp. vii-xxix; A.J.P. Taylor, "Introduction," in Karl Marx and Friedrich Engels, *The Communist Manifesto* (Harmondsworth: Penguin, 1967), pp. 7-47. There are other introductions to the *Manifesto* that fall into the same category of anti-introductions. Francis Randall's introduction to the Washington Square Press edition (1964), for example, placed special emphasis on attacking Marx the person, attributing to him various immoral views, but did not otherwise differ from the account supplied by Beer and Taylor. Among others, Harold Laski (Pantheon), Dirk Struik (International), Leo Huberman and Paul Sweezy (Monthly Review Press), David McLellan (Oxford), and Frederick Bender (Norton) have written introductions/afterwords that are reasonably fair to Marx and more typical of scholarly introductions to classic works generally. For the most comprehensive background, see David Ryazanoff, *The Communist Manifesto of Karl Marx and Friedrich Engels* (New York: International, 1930).

5. Samuel H. Beer, *The City of Reason* (Cambridge, MA: Harvard University Press, 1949), p. 98; A.J.P. Taylor, *From Napoleon to the Second International* (London: Hamish Hamilton, 1993), pp. 379-80.

6. See E.P. Thompson, *The Poverty of Theory and Other Essays* (New York: Monthly Review Press, 1978); and John Bellamy Foster, "Introduction," in Joseph Ferraro, *Freedom and Determination in History According to Marx and Engels* (New York: Monthly Review Press, 1992).

7. Melvin Rader, *Marx's Interpretation of History* (New York: Oxford University Press, 1979), pp. 5-6. For a cogent treatment of the positivistic tendencies of the Second International, see Lucio Colletti, *From Rousseau to Lenin*

(New York: Monthly Review Press, 1972). A classic account of the origins of the philosophy of Soviet Marxism is to be found in Gustav A. Wetter, *Dialectical Materialism* (New York: Praeger, 1958).

8. Marx, *Early Writings* (New York: Vintage, 1974), p. 244.

9. Heraclitus in Matthew Thomas McClure, ed., *The Early Philosophers of Greece* (New York: D. Appleton-Century Company, 1935), pp. 123-25; G.W.F. Hegel, *Phenomenology of Spirit* (New York: Oxford University Press, 1977), p. 11.

10. Hegel, *Hegel's Logic* (New York: Oxford University Press, 1975), pp. 116-17.

11. Marx, *Capital*, Vol. I (New York: Vintage, 1976), p. 103.

12. Bertell Ollman, *Dialectical Investigations* (New York: Routledge, 1993), pp. 15-17; Marx, *Theories of Surplus Value*, Part III (Moscow: Progress Publishers, 1973), p. 491; Marx, *Theories of Surplus Value*, Part II (Moscow: Progress Publishers, 1968), p. 519. See also Hegel, *Hegel's Logic*, p. 174. A key component of Marx's dialectical method lies in discerning the *historical specificity* of any given set of social relations/contradictions; see Karl Korsch, *Karl Marx* (New York: Russell and Russell, 1938).

13. Ellen Meiksins Wood, *Democracy Against Capitalism* (New York: Cambridge University Press, 1995), p. 24.

14. Ibid., pp. 5, 21-22, 29; Marx, "Letter to the Editorial Board of *Ostechestvennye Zapiski,*" in Teodor Shanin, *Late Marx and the Russian Road* (New York: Monthly Review Press, 1983), p. 136; Marx and Engels, *The Communist Manifesto* (New York: Monthly Review Press, 1964), p. 2.

15. Marx, *Preface to a Critique of Political Economy* (see appendix to this volume).

16. Paul Sweezy, "Introduction," *The Theory of Capitalist Development* (New York: Monthly Review Press, 1970), and Marx, "Preface," *Capital* I; and Marx, *Grundrisse* (New York: Vintage, 1973), p. 101.

17. Marx, *Capital* I, p. 280.

18. Ibid, pp. 279-80.

19. Marx, "Wage Labour and Capital," in Marx and Engels, *Collected Works*, Vol. 9 (New York: International Publishers, 1977), p. 226.

20. Marx, *Capital* I, p. 799.

21. Ernest Mandel, *The Formation of the Economic Thought of Karl Marx* (New York: Monthly Review Press, 1971), p. 142.

22. Marx, "Wage Labour and Capital," p. 216; World Bank, *World Development Report, 1990* (New York: Oxford University Press, 1990); Paul Burkett, "Poverty Crisis in the Third World," *Monthly Review*, vol. 42, no. 7 (December 1990): 20-32; Edward N. Wolff, *Top Heavy: A Study of the Increasing Inequality of Wealth in America* (New York: Twentieth Century Fund, 1995), p. 11.

23. David Caute, *Essential Writings of Karl Marx*, p. 217; Spencer quoted in Hal Draper, *Karl Marx's Theory of Revolution*, vol. 3, *The 'Dictatorship of the Proletariat'* (New York: Monthly Review Press, 1986), p. 11.

24. Marx, "Critique of the Gotha Programme," in Marx and Engels, *Selected Works in One Volume* (New York: International Publishers, 1968), pp. 323-25, 330-33; Karl Marx and Frederick Engels, *Writings on the Paris Commune* (New York: Monthly Review Press, 1971), pp. 74-81. For a contemporary Marxist account of the contradiction between the capitalist state apparatus and democratic government see Michael Parenti, "Popular Sovereignty vs. the State," *Monthly Review*, vol. 46, no. 10 (March 1995), pp. 1-16.

25. Marx, quoted in Draper, *Karl Marx's Theory of Revolution*, vol. 3, *The 'Dictatorship of the Proletariat'*, p. 162.

26. Marx, "Confessions," in Shanin, *Late Marx*, p. 140; Marx, "For a Ruthless Criticism of Everything Existing," in Marx and Engels, *The Marx-Engels Reader* (New York: W.W. Norton, 1978), p. 13. For the background to Marx's statement "I am not a Marxist," see Hal Draper, *Karl Marx's Theory of Revolution*, vol. 2, *The Politics of Social Classes* (New York: Monthly Review Press, 1978), pp. 5-11. See also Derek Sayer, *The Violence of Abstraction* (New York: Basil Blackwell, 1987). On Marx and vernacular revolutionary traditions, see Shanin, *Late Marx*, pp. 243-75.

27. See Erich Fromm, "Introduction," in Erich Fromm, ed., *Socialist Humanism* (Garden City, NY: Doubleday, 1965), pp. viii-ix.

Fischer: How To Read Karl Marx

1. *On the Jewish Question* in *Karl Marx: Early Writings*, translated and edited by T.B. Bottomore (London: C.A. Watts, 1963), pp. 24-25.

2. Ibid., p. 26.

3. *Marx-Engels Gesamt-Ausgabe* (MEGA), Vol. I (Berlin, 1932), pp. 99 ff.* See also Loyd D. Easton and Kurt H. Guddat, eds., *Writings of the Young Marx on Philosophy and Society* (Garden City, NY: Doubleday, 1967).

4. *Contribution to the Critique of Hegel's Philosophy of Right* in Bottomore, *Karl Marx: Early Writings*, p. 45.

5. *Economic and Philosophical Manuscripts* in ibid., p. 124.

6. Ibid., p. 126.

7. *Contribution to the Critique of Hegel's Philosophy of Right*, pp. 43-44.

8. *Economic and Philosophical Manuscripts*, in Bottomore, *Karl Marx: Early Writings*, p. 167.

9. *Marx-Engels Werke*, Vol. I (Berlin, 1956), p. 231.*

10. *The German Ideology*, edited by R. Pascal (New York: International Publishers, 1947), pp. 74-75.

11. *Economic and Philosophical Manuscripts*, p. 157.

12. Ibid., pp. 157-58.

13. Ibid., p. 158.

14. Ibid., p. 159.

15. Ibid., p. 153.

16. Ibid., p. 154.

17. Letter to Jenny Marx dated 21 June 1856, in Emile Bottigelli, *Lettres et documents de Karl Marx 1856-1883* (Milan: Feltrinelli, 1958.)*

18. *Economic and Philosophical Manuscripts*, pp. 159-60.

19. Ibid., p. 162.

20. Ibid.

21. Ibid., p. 155.

22. Ibid., p. 176.

23. Grundrisse der Kritik der *Politischen Ökonomie* (Moscow, 1939), p. 539.*

---

* Translations of the entries marked with an asterisk have been supplied by the translator; all others have been taken from published works, as indicated.

24. *Capital* III (Moscow, Foreign Languages Publishing House, 1959), pp. 799-800.
25. *Economic and Philosophical Manuscripts*, p. 202.
26. Ibid., pp. 213-14.
27. Ibid., pp. 127-28.
28. *Capital* I (Moscow: Foreign Languages Publishing House, 1959), pp. 177-78.
29. *Grundrisse*, p. 505.*
30. *Capital* I, pp. 179-80.
31. Ibid., p. 183.
32. Ibid., pp. 183-84.
33. Ibid., p. 351.
34. Ibid., p. 351.
35. *Grundrisse*, p. 390.*
36. *Capital* I, pp. 351-52.
37. *The German Ideology*, pp. 43-44.
38. *Capital* I, p. 363.
39. *The German Ideology*, pp. 46-47.
40. *Capital* I, p. 403.
41. Ibid., p. 420.
42. Ibid., pp. 422-24.
43. Ibid., pp. 486-88.
44. *The German Ideology*, pp. 65-66.
45. Ibid., pp. 22-24.
46. *Grundrisse*, p. 76.*
47. Economic and Philosophical Manuscripts, p. 114.
48. Ibid., p. 134.
49. MEGA, Vol. 3, pp. 535-36.*
50. Ibid., p. 536.*
51. Ibid.*
52. Ibid., pp. 539-40.*
53. *Economic and Philosophical Manuscripts*, p. 125.
54. Ibid., p. 129.
55. *Grundrisse*, pp. 715 ff.*
56. *Economic and Philosophical Manuscripts*, p. 138.
57. Ibid., p. 121.
58. *Capital* I, pp. 35-36.
59. Ibid., pp. 37-38.
60. Ibid., p. 71.
61. Ibid., pp. 72-73.
62. Ibid., p. 77.
63. *Grundrisse*, p. 75.*
64. *Capital* I, pp. 84-85.
65. *Economic and Philosophical Manuscripts*, p. 193.
66. Ibid., pp. 193-94.
67. *The Communist Manifesto* (Moscow: Progress Publishers, 1952), p. 40.
68. Ibid., p. 41.
69. *The German Ideology*, pp. 48-49.
70. *Communist Manifesto*, pp. 43-44.
71. *The Poverty of Philosophy*, (Moscow: Foreign Languages Publishing House, n.d.), p. 137.

72. *Capital* I, pp. 718 ff.
73. *Communist Manifesto*, pp. 53-60.
74. *Capital* III, pp. 862-63.
75. *The Eighteenth Brumaire of Louis Bonaparte*, in *Karl Marx and Frederick Engels: Selected Works*, Vol. I (Moscow: Foreign Languages Publishing House, 1950), p. 249.
76. Ibid., p. 252.
77. Ibid., pp. 305-6.
78. Ibid., pp. 302-3.
79. *The German Ideology*, p. 39.
80. Ibid., p. 40.
81. *Communist Manifesto*, pp. 56-57.
82. *The German Ideology*, p. 41.
83. *Communist Manifesto*, pp. 45-46.
84. Ibid., p. 58.
85. *Capital* I, p. 763.
86. Ibid., p. 763.
87. Preface to *A Contribution to The Critique of Political Economy*, in *Karl Marx and Frederick Engels: Selected Works*, Vol. I, pp. 328-29.
88. *Communist Manifesto*, p. 60.
89. *Capital* I, p. 763.
90. *The Poverty of Philosophy*, p. 122.
91. Ibid., p. 196.
92. *Wage Labor and Capital* in *Selected Works*, Vol. I, p. 83.
93. *Contribution to the Critique of Hegel's Philosophy of Right*, p. 52.
94. *Grundrisse*, p. 111.*
95. *The Future Results of British Rule in India* in *Selected Works*, Vol. I, p. 324.
96. *Capital* I, pp. 18-19.
97. *The Holy Family* (Moscow, Foreign Languages Publishing House, 1956), p. 52.
98. Ibid., p. 125.
99. Letter to Bolte dated 23 November 1871, in *Selected Works*, Vol. II, pp. 423-24.
100. *Capital* III, p. 159.
101. *Letters to Dr Kugelmann* (London, Martin Lawrence), p. 125.
102. *The Eighteenth Brumaire of Louis Bonaparte*, p. 229.
103. Ibid., p. 263.
104. Ibid., p. 225.
105. *The German Ideology*, pp. 28-29.
106. Ibid., pp. 197-98.
107. *The Eighteenth Brumaire of Louis Bonaparte*, p. 225.
108. *Capital* I, pp. 59-60.
109. Ibid., p. 39.
110. Ibid., pp. 39-40.
111. Ibid., p. 44.
112. Ibid., p. 197.
113. Ibid., p. 69.
114. Ibid., p. 86.
115. Ibid., pp. 101-2.
116. Ibid., p. 119.

117. Ibid., p. 122.
118. Ibid., p. 146.
119. Ibid., pp. 151-52.
120. Ibid., pp. 152-53.
121. Ibid., p. 167.
122. Ibid., pp. 168-69.
123. Ibid., pp. 170-71.
124. Ibid., p. 173.
125. Ibid., pp. 193-94.
126. Ibid., p. 204.
127. Ibid., p. 205.
128. Ibid., p. 209.
129. Ibid., p. 217.
130. Ibid., p. 232.
131. Ibid., p. 233.
132. Ibid., pp. 234-35.
133. *Capital* III, p. 37.
134. Ibid., p. 39.
135. Ibid., pp. 42-43.
136. Ibid., pp. 47-48.
137. Ibid., p. 50.
138. Ibid., p. 191.
139. Ibid., p. 807.
140. Ibid., p. 244.
141. Ibid., p. 245
142. Ibid., p. 251.
143. Ibid., pp. 252-54.
144. *Capital* I, p. 713.
145. Ibid., p. 760.
146. *Capital* III, p. 799.
147. *Grundrisse*, p. 231.[*]
148. *Capital* I, p. 645.
149. Ibid., p. 270.
150. Ibid., p. 395.
151. *Wages, Price and Profit* in *Selected Works*, Vol. I, pp. 401-2.
152. *Wage Labor and Capital* in ibid., p. 87.
153. *Capital* I, p. 644.
154. Ibid., p. 645.
155. Preface to *A Contribution to the Critique of Political Economy*, pp. 328-29.
156. *Capital* III, pp. 472-73.
157. *Capital* I, p. 763.
158. *Communist Manifesto*, pp. 48-49.
159. *The Civil War in France* in *Selected Works*, Vol. I, p. 474.
160. *Capital* III, p. 427.
161. Ibid., p. 428.
162. *Communist Manifesto*, pp. 95-96.
163. *Address of the Central Committee to the Communist League* in *Selected Works*, Vol. I, pp. 102, 108.
164. *Communist Manifesto*, p. 12.
165. *Marx-Engels Werke*, Vol. 17, p. 652.[*]

166. *The Poverty of Philosophy*, p. 197.
167. *Communist Manifesto*, pp. 59, 74.
168. *The Eighteenth Brumaire of Louis Bonaparte*, p. 301.
169. Letter to Josef Weydemeyer dated 5 March 1852 in *Selected Works*, Vol. II, p. 410.
170. *The Civil War in France*, pp. 471-72.
171. Engels, *The Housing Question* in *Selected Works*, Vol. I, p. 555.
172. *The Civil War in France*, pp. 471-74.
173. *Critique of the Gotha Programme* in *Selected Works*, Vol. II, p. 30.
174. Ibid., pp. 22-23.
175. *The Holy Family*, pp. 52-53.
176. *Herr Vogt* (Berlin: 1953), p. 75.*
177. *Marx-Engels Werke*, Vol. 8, p. 412.*
178. *Inaugural Address of the Workingmen's International Association* in *Selected Works*, Vol. I, p. 347.
179. Ibid., p. 347.
180. *Ein Komplott gegen die Internationale Arbeiterassoziation* (Brunswick: 1874), p. 22.*
181. Letter to P. Lafargue in *Emile Bottigelli: Lettres et documents de Karl Marx 1856-1883* (Milan: Feltrinelli, 1958), p. 171.
182. *Letters to Dr Kugelmann*, pp. 123-24.
183. *The Civil War in France*, p. 491.
184. Marx/Engels, *Briefe an A. Bebel und andere* (Berlin: 1953), p. 170.*
185. *Theses on Feuerbach* in *The German Ideology*, pp. 197-99.
186. Preface to *A Contribution to The Critique of Political Economy*, pp. 327-31.
187. *The Eighteenth Brumaire of Louis Bonaparte*, pp. 225-28.
188. *Capital* I, Preface to the First German Edition, pp. 7-11.

Sweezy: Marx's Method

1. Georg Lukács, *History and Class Consciousness*. The version cited here is translated from *Geschichte und Klassenbewusstsein* (Berlin: Der Malik-Verlag, 1923).
2. Marx, Preface, first edition, *Capital* Vol. I (Chicago: Charles H. Kerr, 1933), p. 14.
3. David Ricardo, *Principles of Political Economy and Taxation*, E.C.K. Gonner, ed. (London: G. Bell and Sons, 1929), p. 1.
4. Marx, Introduction to *Grundrisse*. The version cited here appeared as Introduction to *A Contribution to a Critique of Political Economy* (Chicago: Charles H. Kerr, 1911), p. 302.
5. Ibid., pp. 303-4. Italics added.
6. *Capital* Vol. III, p. 1025.
7. *Capital* I, p. 707.
8. *Capital* II (Editor's Preface), p. 7.
9. Lukács, *Geschichte und Klassenbewusstsein*, p. 7.
10. Marx, *The Eighteenth Brumaire of Louis Bonaparte* (New York: International, 1963), p. 13.
11. Marx, *The Poverty of Philosophy* (New York: International, 1963).
12. Lukács, *Geschichte und Klassenbewusstsein*, p. 173.

INDEX